UNFUCK YOUR HABITAT

UNFUCK your HABITAT

YOU'RE BETTER THAN YOUR MESS

RACHEL HOFFMAN

ST. MARTIN'S GRIFFIN ❧ NEW YORK

www.stmartins.com

Designed by Richard Oriolo

The Library of Congress Cataloging-in-Publication Data
is available upon request.

ISBN 978-1-250-10295-9 (paper over board)
ISBN 978-1-250-10296-6 (e-book)

Our books may be purchased in bulk for educational,
business, or promotional use. Please contact your local
bookseller or the Macmillan Corporate and Premium Sales
Department at 1-800-221-7945, extension 5442, or by e-mail
at MacmillanSpecialMarkets@macmillan.com.

First Edition: January 2017

10 9 8 7 6 5 4 3 2 1

For Andy,

because you believe I can do anything, I can.

CONTENTS

1 • GETTING STARTED

2 • UNFUCKING YOUR OWN HABITAT

3 • TROUBLESHOOTING: DEALING WITH OTHER PEOPLE IN YOUR FUCKED-UP SPACE

4 • SPECIAL CASES

5 • CONCLUSION

1

GETTING STARTED

NICE ASS, NOW GET OFF IT

Tell me if this sounds familiar: You're flipping through home-organization magazines or browsing on home-improvement and decorating websites, thinking, "This is it. I'm finally doing it. I'm going to get my house under control." You look at picture after glossy picture of perfectly organized spaces, with no visible clutter, clearly labeled storage solutions, and gleaming fresh paint, rooms with sunlight streaming in through the windows, and you think to yourself, "Are you fucking kidding me?"

Those pictures seem impossible. Hell, they *are* impossible if you own enough possessions to function in modern life. You don't live in the world that's being shown in those pictures. You live in the real world. A messy world that's full of dirty dishes, clothes languishing in laundry baskets, and a dining room table you haven't seen the surface of in months. You're not a slob. You just don't have the time, the money, the energy, or even the inclination to achieve what those pictures are showing you. You just want to get your home to the point where a drop-in guest doesn't send you into a tailspin of panic, and where you can live your everyday life without being disgusted or depressed by your surroundings. You know, somewhere deep down, that your home will never look anything like those pictures, and it's depressing, discouraging, and ultimately pretty damn frustrating.

You may be looking at those magazines or websites and thinking that there's no hope for you, and no hope for your home. Your house is never going to look like that. You may be thinking that a clean, organized home is completely out of reach, and there's just no way for it to get better than whatever state of mess it's in right now. You feel trapped by the state of your home, and powerless to do anything about it. Well, good news! **You're wrong.**

There's a universe of difference between a picture-perfect home that can be featured in magazines and a perfectly functional and livable home that you aren't ashamed of or stressed out by. And *Unfuck Your Habitat* can teach you how to have a home you love and feel comfortable in, while helping you realize that your home doesn't need to look like the ones in those pictures in order for you to love living in it.

You deserve better than to live in filth, and with just a little bit of effort and practice, you can easily master the skills and habits you need in order to get and keep your home livable. It's going to take some time, and nothing gets better overnight, but it *will* get better.

Other housekeeping and organizing systems have a specific

kind of person in mind. They assume that everyone is married with kids, with one spouse at home with a lot of time to devote to housekeeping. They tend to ignore single people, or people without kids, or students, or people with pets, or people with roommates, or people with full-time jobs or classes or other shit going on. They ignore people with physical or mental illnesses or other limitations that don't allow for complicated, involved housekeeping on an inflexible schedule. They forget about people who live in apartments, or rented rooms, or a small space in someone else's home. They forget that people live at home with their parents, or in dorm rooms with total strangers. They forget that not everyone fits into a narrow mold of circumstance and ability, and they forget that sometimes . . . you just don't feel like it. Basically, they ignore a whole lot of people who live in the real world.

Since so few of us fit the mold of these traditional housekeeping systems, it doesn't make sense to try to follow those methods and expect them to lead us to success. A picture-perfect showroom home is admirable, but, let's be honest, that's not going to be a reality for most of us. And that's okay! So the first step in turning our messes into something we can happily live with is realizing that it's time to rethink the way we approach housekeeping and organizing and how they fit into the lives we actually live.

In this book, you'll learn how to incorporate cleaning and organizing into a busy life, and how to work with all of the various fun things life throws at you that have kept you from doing this up to now. You'll learn that rather than be intimidated by what you think other people's homes look like, you can get to a point where you're happy and comfortable with what your own home can be. You'll realize that the real world rarely, if ever, lines up with what aspirational magazines and websites are showing you. It's not as intimidating as it seems, but I'm willing to bet no one's ever broken it down into a system that works in your world, and so it's easier just to write it off as completely impossible . . . and then never even get started. And that's why you are where you are right now: overwhelmed, discouraged, feeling like a failure, and hating your home.

We should probably start by accepting the fact that, for the most part, cleaning your house kind of sucks. Sorry, but it does. Getting and keeping your house clean and organized isn't necessarily difficult, but it's rarely fun, and we all have other things we'd rather be doing. If given a choice, very few people would choose to spend their time cleaning or organizing their home. It seems like a giant time investment, during which your life is totally devoid of fun and sunshine and anything else you like. But there's no reason tidying up your home has to take up all of your precious spare time. It can be accomplished just a little bit at a time, in between the far more enjoyable and important things that happen in your life. It's critical to realize that you aren't beyond hope. **You can always improve your living situation, but you need to do some work to get there.**

We're often busy, and sometimes we're lazy. No need to sugarcoat that. But wouldn't it be nice to walk into your house at the end of a busy day and not feel depressed or disgusted or dejected? There are very few people who enjoy cleaning on a regular basis (and frankly, I'm a little suspicious of those people anyway). So let's just accept that it's not necessarily going to be the most interesting or fulfilling part of your day and move on to actually getting it done so that you can finally do the things you *want* to do in a home that you don't hate spending time in.

Once you've acquired the tools you need to keep your house from devolving into a total shithole while still managing to do the things you enjoy, you'll develop a habit of keeping your living space nice without it taking over your life. You'll find that you can maintain a home that doesn't stress you out or embarrass you, and you can accomplish that in only a few minutes a day. You'll be able to have people over if you want to. You won't panic over unannounced guests.

The important thing to remember is that there is nothing that can't be unfucked with a little bit of effort and motivation. You just have to do it. You have to overcome the compulsion to sit on the couch and mess around on the computer or watch TV, and get up and do something. Anything. If you have the motivation but lack the ability, you have to figure out how to work with or around any limitations that have prevented you from doing this in the past. Unfuck Your Habitat (or UfYH) is all about helping you do just that. It's about lighting a gentle fire under our asses and reminding ourselves that we deserve a home we can be comfortable in and proud of. It's about acquiring the skills we lack and applying those skills in our everyday lives in a way that results in improvement without burnout. It's about celebrating every success, no matter how small it might seem at the time. Because when we accomplish something, especially something that seemed impossible, it feels pretty awesome.

WHO NEEDS UNFUCK YOUR HABITAT?

So many different kinds of people have been failed by traditional housekeeping and organizational systems. In fact, I'd be willing to bet that close to an entire generation has entered adulthood without the skills needed to keep a clean and organized home—skills that previous generations took for granted. Whereas in the stereotypical nuclear family of the past, one of the parents (usually the mother) would teach housekeeping skills to the next generation (usually the daughters), the realities of life today don't make this a feasible, realistic, or desirable scenario. The definition of "family" is evolving all the time, but that archaic mindset regarding housekeeping roles hasn't changed much at all. As a result, many domestic skills have fallen by the wayside due to lack of time, shifting priorities, or inadequate tools. As we move past traditional roles within the home into structures that better fit how we actually live our lives, we also need to adapt our methods for keeping our homes running smoothly. As a society, we haven't yet caught up to that reality, so we've lost a whole lot of our ability to get the job done while we've been looking around wondering whose job it is.

Traditional housekeeping systems attempt to make people's lives fit into a rigid structure of routines and schedules for cleaning and maintaining the house, and that doesn't make any sense at all for a lot of people. Doesn't it make more sense to fit your cleaning routines around your life instead? Today, it's critical to incorporate flexible routines that work with your life instead of against it; otherwise nothing will ever get done. Trying to use a housekeeping system that was developed for someone with a very different lifestyle is a little like wearing shoes that are two sizes too small: It's uncomfortable, it's awkward, and pretty soon, you're going to get frustrated and give up entirely, left feeling much worse than when you started. So maybe it's time to try something completely different—something that was designed to work for people who are failed by other systems and that recognizes that you have a whole lot of other shit going on.

So, who needs *Unfuck Your Habitat*?

EVERYONE, REGARDLESS OF GENDER

With all the different living situations that we enjoy today, assigning housekeeping tasks based on archaic and outdated gender roles just doesn't make sense. Traditional standards of who "should" be doing the cleaning don't apply to how people live their lives nowadays, and haven't for quite some time. Households are made up of every combination of gender, age, and relationship.

If you live somewhere, you deserve for that place to be nice and clean and livable, and you should be the one who makes it that way. If several people are responsible for making the mess, each of those people is responsible for getting it clean and under control. It doesn't matter who you are or what box or boxes you check. Gender roles as they relate to cleaning are bullshit,* and just offer a handy excuse for half the population to be lazy and the other half to feel guilty.

BUSY PEOPLE

We're all busy. Very busy, in fact. Almost all of us have stuff going on that takes up a vast majority of our time, whether it's work, school, family obligations, or anything else. It doesn't make sense for us to follow a bunch of steps that were developed for people who have hours each day to devote to cleaning and organizing their home. Who actually has that? No one I know. Even the people I know who are home all day, whether they work at home or are stay-at-home parents, don't have time for the type of strict structure outlined by traditional systems because they're busy doing the million little things necessary for keeping the rest of their lives running smoothly. To be honest, cleaning and organizing the house falls so far down on the list of things to do that it often falls off that list entirely. We haven't adapted how we look at housekeeping to reflect how we really live our lives, and that's why so many of us feel like we're failing at it. With UfYH, you'll learn how to change the way cleaning and other home-related tasks fit into your life, and be able to adapt and adjust to whatever life throws at you at any given time.

* See page 14 for more on *this*.

PEOPLE TOO BROKE TO HAVE A FULL-TIME MAID (SO, YOU)

One of the other things that most organizational and cleaning systems have in common is that they tend to require a significant investment, either of money or of time. And if you're like most other people these days, you don't exactly have a surplus of either one. Any free time or extra money is almost immediately earmarked for something else, something that's more important or possibly more fun. So you may find yourself wondering if it's even possible to get your shit under control if you can't spend a ton of money or every waking moment dealing with your mess, because everything you're seeing and reading sure makes it seem like it's not. It *is* possible, and UfYH will show you how. There's no reason that getting your home in order should drain your bank account or your energy reserves.

ANYONE WITH PHYSICAL OR MENTAL ILLNESSES OR DISABILITIES

Many people come to UfYH because they can't find a place for themselves in the expectations of other systems. For example, people with mental or physical illnesses or limitations often find that massive cleaning sessions or inflexible schedules involving intense bursts of work just aren't physically possible. It's not about being lazy; it's about not being able to accomplish what ends up being a bunch of impossible tasks because of factors that are *entirely beyond your control.* The underlying assumption about people's ability to do housework seems to be that everyone is able-bodied with plenty of energy to spare. That assumption can be pretty damaging, because everyone who doesn't fit into that tiny little box simply gets left behind. UfYH realizes that not everyone fits this mold, and will help show you how to work within or around whatever your limitations may be.

PEOPLE ON THEIR OWN FOR THE FIRST TIME

Young adults in their first living situation away from their parents—whether that's a dorm, apartment, or shared housing of any kind—often find themselves at a loss as far as what to do, how to do it, and when it should be done when it comes to housework. And if you grew up in an environment where you didn't learn these skills, either because your parents weren't good at keeping a house or because they did it all for you and never made you learn, being out on your own can be a bit of a startling wake-up call. There's nothing inherently wrong with not knowing what to do around the house, but the skills needed have to be learned at some point, and the longer you wait, the more difficult it can be.

LAZY PEOPLE

Then there are some of us who actually *are* lazy. And that's totally fine! We all have a lot going on in our lives, and when faced with a little bit of down time, it's totally understandable that the last thing you feel like doing is housework. I mean, doing the dishes takes a lot of energy, and it's not fun at all, so it's really no wonder that so many people choose to just succumb to the inclination to sit down and do nothing. The problem with this is that, well, house stuff needs to happen at some point. If you let it go forever because you just don't feel like it, your house is quickly going to become (and stay) a messy disaster. So while laziness is a completely understandable reason not to work on getting your home in order, you need to get past it for even just a short amount of time. And then you can go back to doing whatever it is you'd prefer to be doing, even if that happens to be nothing at all.

PERFECTIONISTS

It seems counterintuitive, but some people who identify as perfectionists tend to have trouble keeping their home in order. Because it's so difficult to clean and organize everything thoroughly and perfectly all at once, perfectionists can get discouraged by what seems like a lack of results, and just give up. Learning that progress is incremental and not necessarily flawless can be a huge step toward getting a messy house under control, a little bit at a time.

THERE'S NO END to the reasons that people don't or can't clean their home, and there's no one type or category of person who needs help with housekeeping. Lots of people in lots of situations find themselves not up to the task of keeping their home in order. Whether that's due to a shortage of time, a lack of skills, physical limitations, or a loss of motivation, there is hope. With practice, focus, and, most important, a solid but flexible game plan, everyone can get their mess under control, and transform their home from something they're embarrassed and stressed out by into something that's comfortable and calm.

And About This Gender-Role Bullshit . . .

As we've already discussed, there are a whole bunch of reasons why someone might not know what to do in order to keep a clean home. One of the reasons that's unfortunately all too common is that a lot of people still buy into the idea that cleaning a home and maintaining a household is "women's work." Meaning, they think men are automatically off the hook for housework simply because they're men.

A very common (but especially obnoxious) assertion is that "men just don't see the mess the same way women do." This is an infuriating viewpoint that, unfortunately, lots and lots of people believe. Like, *so* many people. This tired old trope is meant to "explain" why men often don't do their fair share of housework and why all of those domestic responsibilities generally fall to women. And it's complete bullshit. Everyone sees the mess. There's just a huge number of people who believe it's not a man's job to do anything about it.

Before we dive too deep into a discussion of gender roles and expectations and how they get all wrapped up with household duties, there are a few things to keep in mind. First, it isn't true that men are bad at housekeeping and women are good at it. I can name dozens of examples from my own experience that contradict that (I'm sure you can, too). What we *can* say, however, is that we are at least somewhat socially conditioned to see those roles as the default, and anyone who doesn't fit into them as an exception to the rule. Also, we should remember that this mindset is fundamentally traditional and heteronormative and not 100 percent applicable in modern life. The typical "nuclear family" (Mom, Dad, and a couple of kids) is less and less common now, with families and households instead being made up in endless configurations that don't fall within those very stringent, very traditionally defined parameters. So when we challenge our perceptions of those gender roles, we also need to challenge how we define "family" and "household" and make some adjustments to accurately reflect reality.

That said, the idea that men are not good at housekeeping is a really pervasive societal perception that has infiltrated almost every aspect of modern life. Advertising, TV shows, gender-directed media like magazines, and irritating social media memes all reinforce the "fact" that men just don't do housework. Or that if they try, they're hilariously inept at it and need a woman to set them straight and do it right. Or that a wife's or a mom's job is to keep the house clean, regardless of her job or responsibilities outside the home, even though she may have as many professional demands on her time as her male partner, if not more. Or that a bachelor's home is expected to be a disaster (that is, until his mom comes and cleans it up, or he finds a girlfriend to give his place "a woman's touch"). And every time we repeat these stereotypes or accept them as fact, we not only help advance these outdated gender norms and place an unearned burden on women, but we also demean and infantilize men by tacitly accepting that they just don't or can't do housework.

Lots of men—especially those raised with more traditional upbringings like that nuclear family we were just talking about—see a mess, figure it'll get taken care of soon, and then cease thinking about it at all. Lots of women see the same mess, figure they'll need to take care of it soon, and start trying to figure out how to make that happen. See the difference? Women are conditioned to see dirt and messes as their responsibility to clean up, and men are conditioned to see dirt and messes in a way that requires no further action on their part. It's the *interpretation* of what they're seeing, not whether they actually see it. So it's not accurate to say that "men don't see the mess." It's bullshit.

It's what happens after the mess is observed that matters: Is it our job to do something about that mess, or are we just passively observing it with the expectation that someone else is going to take care of it?

Once again, I'm not saying that men are terrible at housework and women are good at it. That would be just as ridiculous as saying that men are incapable of seeing messes just because they're men. Tons of men are great at housework, and tons of women are terrible at it, and most people, regardless of gender, fall somewhere in between. Many households have an easy and equitable division of labor, unrestrained by gender roles, and they're doing just fine. Gender-based housework is clearly, then, not any kind of biological imperative, but a social one. We each have our own natural tendencies, but those tendencies are influenced by everyday social cues and expectations.

No one is born knowing how to do housework. We all have to learn it somehow. Some people learn it by being taught within their home by parents, siblings, or other family members at an early age. Other people figure it out on their own through trial and error when they first start living outside the family home. Still others teach themselves through reading, research, and observation (which also includes a fair amount of trial and error). The point is, there's no innate housekeeping gene that's only passed on to girls. Everyone has the same ability and capacity to learn these skills.

And it's considerably easier to learn at a young age. By starting young, children grow up with the necessary habits for keeping a home clean, and learn the basic skills that will help them keep their mess under control for the rest of their lives. So that's why, within the family home, it's so important to teach all children these skills, regardless of gender and age. Anyone who grows up with these skills is at an advantage over those of us who need to learn them later on, since kids tend to learn things with an ease that most of us adults don't possess. Not to mention that being brought up in a household where everyone is expected to carry their fair share goes a long way to normalizing the idea that housework is for everyone.

In addition, there's no small amount of learned helplessness associated with gender roles and cleaning. Let's go back to those god-awful social media memes and eye-rollingly terrible TV commercials poking fun at how men are just hopeless around the house. They don't know how to do laundry! Isn't that hilarious? (No. It's not.) All those dramatized examples of how they can't get their own children clean, fed, and dressed, and how the smallest routine task leads to catastrophe or slapstick comedy. And how a woman needs to swoop in and fix it, effortlessly, while chuckling about how endearing it all is, instead of fast-pitching a bottle of glass cleaner across the room in frustration and anger, which is a much more likely real-world reaction to that much obnoxious learned helplessness.

Going hand in hand with learned helplessness is the concept of strategic incompetence. Picture being asked or expected to do something you really hate—for example, the dishes. So you kind of half-ass the job because you hate it, and the dishes don't really get all that clean. Then the person who asked you to do the dishes gets exasperated and ends up rewashing them and never asks you to do them again. Which is totally what you wanted in the first place, right? Well, that works out pretty well for you, but it's a shitty thing to do to the person who wants and needs you to do your part. It's not that you don't know how to or physically can't complete the task competently; you're being crappy at it so that you won't be expected to do it again. And that's not a great thing to do to someone. It's fundamentally selfish. Sometimes we have to do things we don't enjoy because it's part of living in a home, and pretending to suck at something so you won't have to do it again is just rude.

I mean, are we serious about teaching people to believe that if you do something terribly enough, you'll never be expected to do it again? I hope we all realize how absurd that is. When children are learning how to do things, we don't take one imperfect attempt as a failure and cease expecting them to acquire that skill forever. We expect them to keep trying until they get it right. This isn't a cycle that's only applicable to children. If you can't do something well, you keep doing it until you can. You use what resources you can find to get better at it. You don't just shrug it off with "Oh, well. I'm terrible at this and should therefore never be expected to try again." Come *on*. We're doing men (and anyone else who's new to acquiring these skills) an incredible disservice when we accept this as some kind of fact, letting it stand that we think they're somehow not capable of acquiring and perfecting new skills.

Any discussion of gender roles, norms, and expectations invariably gets people's hackles up, making them feel attacked, stereotyped, or belittled. So it's very important to realize that all of this isn't necessarily the fault of any individual person, and it certainly doesn't apply across the board. Whether or not someone, or someone's family, significant other, or peer group, buys into or believes these gender stereotypes, the fact remains that they exist and they're shoved down our throats and subconsciously embedded in our brains at every given opportunity. How many men get praised or acknowledged for doing things that women do thanklessly all the time? By giving the impression that it's remarkable when a man completes the basic tasks of domestic living, we're reinforcing the fact that we, as a society, think that this is unusual. That men should be congratulated for doing "women's work." That women are "lucky" when their partner does half of the domestic work. It's almost irrelevant if the people who are involved actually believe this, because *society* believes it. Why do we accept the idea that it's noteworthy when someone cleans up a mess they helped make? Silly, right?

Since we don't live in the '50s anymore (thank goodness), these days, women are just as likely to be working outside the home as men are. In the past, it may have been true that women spent less time and had fewer responsibilities outside the house, and that's why all of the domestic responsibilities fell to them, but it's not true anymore, and it hasn't been for quite some time. Yet we look at a man who works forty-plus hours a week at a high-pressure job, and a woman who works the same number of hours at a similarly stressful job, and we still expect that the woman is going to be the one who puts in all of the additional time to do the housework. We seriously need to step back and examine why that is. The circumstances that led to those expectations no longer exist, but the expectations themselves remain, and any deviation from them is still seen as unusual.

Even knowing where all of these assumptions stem from, there's no getting around the fact that we think of housework and most other domestic tasks as "women's work." And it's plain to see, reinforced in hundreds of insidious ways, that as we regard domestic work as "women's work," we devalue it in a way that says some uncomfortable things about not just how we view the importance of domestic work but how we view the importance of the people who perform it. Traditionally, cleaning and cooking and all the other tasks that make up running a household are performed by women, not only in their own home but also in the workplace. If I tell you to picture a housekeeper, I'm reasonably sure that whatever your mental picture is, it begins with a woman. And these jobs, unpaid in the home, are almost always low-wage, low-prestige jobs out in the workforce as well. And when we don't see a job as valuable, over time we also tend to think of it as easy or nonskilled, even though anyone who performs domestic work for a living or at home can tell you it's not easy at all.

It's time for us to change the way we look at domestic work and the people who perform it. By seeing and acknowledging the amount of labor involved, we can start to realize that a more equal division of labor in our own homes is inherently fairer than expecting it all to fall under the umbrella of "women's work." Domestic and emotional labor like housecleaning, child-rearing, household management (bill paying, grocery shopping, etc.), and the endless other tasks involved in running a household are labor, unpaid but critical to everyday life. These tasks are not the default responsibility of one gender or the other, just as financial contributions and major household decisions are no longer granted solely to one family member just because of his role within the household. In an equitable home, housework is the responsibility of every person who lives there, unless all parties have agreed otherwise.

It's well beyond time to expect everyone to contribute to the domestic aspects of their own household, to expect everyone to acquire the skills necessary to keep a home, and to stop expecting that all domestic responsibilities should automatically fall to one member of the household just because of gender. It's well beyond time to stop buying into this bullshit and to start making our households functional and happy, with all tasks divided up fairly.

THE CASE FOR 20/10s

MARATHON CLEANING AND WHY IT'S A BAD IDEA

When faced with a messy home, most people who aren't predisposed to be domestically competent tend to do the same thing: Wait for it to get to the point where you absolutely cannot stand to look at it for one more second, and then spend a day or two or three cleaning like a maniac until it's livable again. Then you wait for it to get to the worst point again and do the same thing a few weeks or months later, doing mostly nothing in between. This is what we call "marathon cleaning," and it doesn't work. It just doesn't. Why not? Well, a few reasons:

- **IT'S ALL OR NOTHING.** For a few days, you work your ass off and have a completely clean home, but then you do absolutely nothing for days or weeks or months. In the meantime, your home is getting progressively worse and worse until it hits the lowest point before you decide to do something about it again.

- **MARATHONS CAN BE UNHEALTHY.** Many people manifest anxiety or manic episodes with marathon cleaning. This isn't ideal, because you're only cleaning when you're not in a good headspace, and you begin to associate the act of cleaning with being sick or mentally distressed. When cleaning becomes a symptom or a result of your mental state, you tend to wrap it up in way too much emotion, and it becomes an activity fraught with negative associations.

- **IT'S NOT SUSTAINABLE.** You can't use marathons as a way of maintaining a clean house if you're a busy person, because there's just not enough time to spend hours a day cleaning up the shit. And on the rare day that you do have that kind of time to spend, the odds of you spending it all cleaning are pretty slim.

- **IT'S TEMPORARY.** Your house is only clean for a few days at a time, at most. The rest of the time, you're living in mess or filth and not doing anything to improve it, because it hasn't gotten "bad" enough. You tend to focus on the very short period of time after everything is all cleaned up, and forget about the incrementally increasing disaster for the rest of the time.

- **MARATHONS DON'T HELP YOU BUILD HABITS.** Things get really awful, you marathon, and then you wait for them to get bad again. In between, you aren't doing anything to help yourself sustain a clean environment. Doing a little bit at frequent intervals is a much more useful habit than spending hours cleaning everything with a really long time in between.

I think it's safe to say that most people approach housekeeping with a marathon state of mind, and this is primarily why so many of our homes are complete messes. Why would you spend time cleaning your house if it's not completely terrible, right? Well, that's dangerous thinking right there. Because our goal is to not have a terrible house for the majority of the time. Our goal is to keep a relatively clean and livable house with a minimal amount of effort, both on a daily basis and for the "big cleans"; you know, when you find out that your landlord or parents or favorite movie star is dropping by for a visit. Ideally, you'll get to a place where those "surprise" visits will be easily dealt with in a very short amount of time without any real stress or anxiety on your part. Hell, if everything goes right, someone could just ring your doorbell unannounced (although, how rude, right?) and you could have them in for a visit without the slightest hesitation or freakout.

Does that sound impossible? If so, that's completely OK. Right now, your home is probably in a state of chaos that you can't picture digging out from under anytime soon. And that's fine. That's normal. That's why you're looking around for a better solution. Looking at the bigger picture of your home as a whole is almost always going to be overwhelming, and when you're overwhelmed, getting started seems like an impossible proposition. It seems even more impossible if you're approaching it with the mindset of marathon cleaning, because you see a big mess and assume it means a big cleanup that takes a lot of time and energy and will leave you exhausted and with no time left for anything else.

When you look at a whole-house mess, you're focusing entirely on the big picture. Everything is a disaster. It all needs to be done. Well, there's no rule saying it all needs to be done at the same time. In order to keep from feeling like the project is too big to handle, you need to step away from that big picture and turn a critical eye to small sections at a time. Small sections are far less terrifying to consider, and reordering your thinking so you can do one or two small areas and then stop will help you to build the skills you need to get your home clean—and to keep it that way without driving yourself up a wall.

MINI-CHALLENGE

- Take a picture of a flat space near you (counter, desk, table, etc.). This is your "before" picture of this space. Now move just five things off of that space and put them back where they belong. That's it. You're one step closer to your "after" already.

WHAT'S A 20/10?

So how do you avoid marathon cleaning but still end up with a clean house? By breaking your tasks down into manageable chunks of time, which we call 20/10s. A 20/10 is twenty minutes of cleaning, followed by a ten-minute break. **The break is not optional.** Breaks are important for a number of reasons, mainly to show that you can stop when you need or want to, and also because they interrupt the part of your thought process that wants to turn a cleaning session into a marathon. So while you might still take several hours to accomplish a task or project, you're breaking it up into workable chunks that allow you to do other, more enjoyable things in between so you don't get lost in and overwhelmed by your task.

20/10s are the heart of the Unfuck Your Habitat system. Every household task can be broken down into 20/10s. How many you need to do is determined by the size of the task; a large project may require many of them, broken up over several days' worth of work. One of the good things about 20/10s is that you can decide how many you want to do at any given time. Had a long day at work and really don't feel like having to spend a lot of time maintaining your house? One or two 20/10s will keep things neater without driving you completely over the edge. Have a room that needs a total overhaul and have a few days to devote to it? You can do as many 20/10s in a row as you need in order to complete your task.

Twenty minutes is not a long time. It requires a minimum time investment on your part, but I can almost guarantee you'll be surprised with how much you can accomplish in such a short chunk of time. It's also much easier to convince yourself to get started when you know that there's an end in sight, and that it's not very far away. Marathon cleaning sessions, while satisfying, are exhausting and make you never want to clean ever again. Twenty minutes at a time, once or a few times a day, is a sustainable way of keeping your habitat unfucked. You can incorporate twenty minutes a day into the rest of your life without feeling like you're spending all of your limited and precious free time cleaning your damn house.

When you look at your entire messy, disorganized house, it's intimidating as hell. Cleaning up seems like an impossible undertaking, and the thought of getting started can be paralyzing because there's rarely an end in sight. By only working in twenty-minute increments, you train yourself to stop looking at the big picture and to break down what you have to do into small, manageable tasks. Reorganizing your thinking in this way is helpful because you don't see a huge, overwhelming challenge that would take days or weeks to accomplish; instead, you see a series of smaller chunks of time that each has a definite beginning and a definite end and can realistically be completed without making you feel like you're devoting every waking moment to cleaning.

A great thing about 20/10s is that you can mess around with them until you find the timing that works best for you. If 20/10s don't feel quite right to you, maybe a 45/15 is more your speed. People with mobility or energy limitations who can't do twenty minutes at a time may find that a 5/15 works without being more than they can handle. Keep playing around with it until you find whatever work/break interval works for you. I'll refer to 20/10s throughout this book, but feel free to substitute whatever your preferred variation is. **Remember, flexible and adaptable for your life; that's our goal.**

It's also likely that most tasks will take far less time than you may have thought. Often we'll put off doing something around the house because of how long we're assuming it'll take. Sometimes you'll find that something you've been dreading and avoiding can be completed in just one or two 20/10s. Even major projects rarely end up requiring the time investment that we assume.

MINI-CHALLENGE

- **Let's give that flat surface from before just one 20/10, starting now. When you're done with that, take a picture. This is your first "after" shot. Congratulations!**

EFF THAT: EFFORT VS. EFFICIENCY

The reason 20/10s are effective is that they provide noticeable results with a limited amount of effort. Marathon cleaning sessions are so terrible in part because you're expending so much energy for such an extended period of time that it feels like no matter what the results are, they're not worth the amount of effort you've put into them. With a 20/10, your effort is intentionally limited; with just twenty minutes of work, you're unlikely to wear yourself out before you start seeing results.

Training yourself to be effective without a huge amount of effort can be difficult. We tend to think of success as directly proportional to the amount of effort we expend, so that unless we're working really, really hard, we think we're not accomplishing anything at all. After just one twenty-minute cleaning session, though, you'll almost definitely have obvious improvement—success!—so it's clear that your effectiveness at getting your shit cleaned up isn't necessarily determined by the amount of effort you put in. It may not seem like twenty minutes will get you very far on a mountain of dishes, but I guarantee the effect will be noticeable. Twenty minutes can be enough time to put away one or two whole loads of clean laundry, or to take a bathroom from horrifying to habitable.

When facing a whole-house clean, our brains will almost always go straight to thinking that we need to marathon it until everything is done, and most people's response to that is a resounding "Eff that." There's absolutely nothing appealing or motivating about marathon cleaning. It's overwhelming and exhausting just to think about, let alone actually do. Facing down just twenty minutes of work, though, is a lot easier. Having a predetermined end point to your effort really does quite a lot toward discouraging the "eff that" response. You're far more likely to actually do the work when you know it's not going to completely wipe you out. And that's the beauty of 20/10s: You can do pretty much anything for just twenty minutes if you know that at the end of it, not only can you stop, but you get to take a break for the sole purpose of rewarding yourself for that twenty minutes of work. It's like the perfect combination of effort, effectiveness, and reward without being exhausted and frustrated at the end of it all. Win/win!

MENTAL HEALTH AND YOUR MESS

One reason some popular housekeeping systems fail is that they rarely take into account how real people live their lives. People living with physical disabilities, chronic illnesses, mental illnesses, or chronic pain often find that the steps laid out for them to get their messes under control are unrealistic. The underlying assumptions behind so many housekeeping systems tend to exclude anyone who isn't able-bodied and healthy in every way. But here in the real world, we have lots of shit going on, and it's necessary to acknowledge that and work with it, rather than ignore the day-to-day reality that so many people are living.

It's all well and good for a book or website to set up detailed lists of what needs to get done when, but if you're not feeling up to it, those lists might as well tell you to strap rockets to your shoes and fly to the moon, because it's just not going to happen. There are days when you just won't be able to get out of bed, or when you're in too much pain to stand for more than a few minutes. Getting your house clean and keeping it that way when you're dealing with any of this stuff means you need to be able to work around all of the bullshit life is throwing in your way. It absolutely can be done; it's just difficult to find resources that tell you how.

And looking at all these lists and pictures and meticulously organized spaces can be incredibly overwhelming and discouraging on the days when you're struggling just to brush your teeth. None of these suggestions take into account the actual circumstances of your life, so why bother? Why set yourself up for failure? Even looking at these schedules and lists can make you feel like a failure when you know you just can't do what they're asking of you. Rather than beating yourself up for not attaining impossible goals, doesn't it make more sense to give yourself goals that you have some chance in hell of being able to accomplish? Work with your life, not against it.

EXCUSES VS. REASONS

One of the UfYH mantras is **"Excuses are boring."** It's used as a preemptive defense against the never-ending number of flimsy excuses offered up for why someone can't do this task or that. (Let's be honest; it's almost always about making the bed.) And when you're living with a mental illness, physical disability, chronic illness, or chronic pain, you likely have an interesting and unhealthy relationship with the word "excuses." So let's break that down before we go any further.

So often, people who have physical limitations on what they can accomplish are told that those limitations are being used as excuses. The notion that people use very real conditions or circumstances simply as an excuse to not do housework is a little ridiculous and not just a little unfair. It's really important not to confuse excuses with reasons. Excuses are things that people use to justify not doing something because *they don't* want *to do it*. Reasons are how people explain not doing something because *they aren't* able *to do it*. See the difference? Saying you don't want to wash the dishes because they're just going to get dirty again later is an excuse. Saying that you can't stand up for more than a few consecutive minutes to wash dishes because you're having a pain flare-up is a reason. So when I say, "Excuses are boring," I'm really talking about those things you throw out there as justification because you just don't want to do whatever it is. I am absolutely not talking about valid, legitimate reasons that prevent you from doing things. But be sure you're being honest with yourself about which is which.

When we start to recognize what's an excuse and what's a reason, maybe we can start to let go of some of the guilt and self-recrimination (to say nothing of the judgment imposed by others) that's associated with the difficulties so many people have doing housework because of disability or illness. So before letting yourself slip too far into negativity about your situation, take a moment to really think about why you aren't doing it, and whether it's due to factors that are largely beyond your control. If so, let go of "lazy" and "excuses" and "not trying hard enough" or any of the other negative things that can cross your mind or your lips when facing the reality of your home and your ability to deal with it.

CLEANLINESS ≠ GODLINESS

There's so much judgment and rhetoric wrapped up in how people view messy homes and the people who live in them. Everyone's quick to label people "lazy" or "slobs," to wonder how they could live that way or why they just can't get their shit together and clean up. It's not always that simple. Messiness is not a moral failing. For some people, it's simply not possible to clean and organize an entire room from top to bottom in one day. It has nothing to do with their value as a person, and everything to do with the various things that they're working with in their lives.

How often have you heard "Cleanliness is next to godliness"? That seems a little extreme, doesn't it? Cleanliness, not kindness or compassion? That's ridiculous, right? But the fact remains that so many people see someone who's messy and make all sorts of assumptions about that person—about their life, about their personality, about their ethics, even about their worth. We need to learn to separate the state of our homes from our feelings of worth. Having a clean home doesn't make you a better person. It just makes you a person with a clean home. Having a messy home, then, doesn't make you a bad person. It doesn't mean you're lazy, or disgusting, or less of a human being than someone whose linen closet looks like a store display.

All of this judgment surrounding cleaning can be completely counterproductive. The more we feel like we're bad or lesser people because of what our homes look like, the less likely we are to do anything about it. There's very little worse than feeling like nothing you do is going to be good enough, and when this moralizing gets attached to the cleanliness of our homes, we might feel like there's no point in trying to improve at all. There's no motivation to make any improvement if you feel like no matter what you do, you're still going to be criticized and looked down on. There's no sense in attempting any level of progress if you're being insulted and belittled (either generally or specifically) by people who assign negative personality characteristics without knowing the specifics of someone's situation. We should, as a whole, be better than that, and sometimes we just aren't.

There are all sorts of reasons why someone might be messy, and laziness is only one of them. If you grew up in a messy house, you might never have learned how to clean. If you have a physical or mental illness or disability, you might physically not be able to clean your house from top to bottom. You might work two jobs and go to school and have no spare time to vacuum. Everyone's situation is different, and they're all valid.

What's important to know, however, is that you totally can work with or around whatever's going on in your life. If you have no free time, well, 20/10s are great, and if you can't manage that, a 5/the-rest-of-the-day can help more than you think, too. If you have physical limitations, there are ways to adapt your housework so that you can do it while taking care of yourself and your health. There's no need to let outside judgment limit what you can do in your own home. All those judgey, moralizing people have no idea what you're living with, so why the hell are you letting them make you feel like crap about your home? It's not about anyone else. It's about you: what you're living with, how you deal with it, how it affects your home.

So let's explore some of the more common mental roadblocks to cleaning up, and some of the ways you can work with or around them to keep your home in order.

DEPRESSION

Why are our minds and our messes so closely linked? One problem is that we tend to let our mess define us. When our home is messy, we see it as a reflection on our worth as a person. It's a really common way of thinking, but it's entirely bullshit. You're more than your mess. But even though our mess doesn't—or shouldn't—define us, it absolutely can affect us. When you're not in a great state of mind, a messy home can exacerbate that. Depression and a messy home are a self-perpetuating cycle that sometimes feels completely impossible to interrupt. (More on this cycle a little later.)

Depression has a way of insinuating itself into every corner of your life, even the ones that seem like they shouldn't have anything to do with mental health. And your living environment is a big part of that. When you feel like crap, there's a good chance your home is going to reflect that. The trouble is, it can be close to impossible to dredge up the energy to tidy up when it's a battle to simply pick your head up off the pillow.

When you're in the midst of a depressive episode, cleaning your house comes in on the List of Things You Want to Do somewhere after taunting a hive of bees and tap-dancing on live television. Everything is just awful. It's a struggle to walk to the bathroom. Making dinner seems more impossible than advanced calculus. Getting out of bed is a vague, distant dream that seems like it may never come true. Meanwhile, the mess gets worse and worse. It seems impossible that you're contributing to this, since that would require some sort of energy on your part. But the mess *is* getting worse, and not only can you not figure out how that's happening, you sure as hell can't figure out how to try to make it better, because of that whole "no energy to spare to even think about it" problem. If you do feel like expending any energy toward doing anything at all, you're more likely to try to feed yourself or, by some miracle, take a shower rather than doing the dishes.

So you're already feeling crappy, and then you look around your messy house, and you start to feel even worse. You feel more depressed, because now you're exhausted and hopeless and can't pull yourself out of bed, and on top of that, your house is a shithole. Which makes you feel useless on top of everything you were already feeling, and then probably overwhelmed on top of that, and quite frankly, having that many feelings at once during a depressive episode is horrible and exhausting and paralyzing. So your depression gets worse, and your mess gets worse, and the two keep feeding on each other and it seems like there's no end in sight.

Good news, though! You can interrupt it. Don't get me wrong, it kind of sucks a little bit, but it can be done. The hardest part is finding the motivation. We've talked about 20/10s, but I'm willing to bet that even that seems a little bit impossible right now, sort of like all of those detailed lists and schedules. It's more than you can handle, and that's totally fine. **Remember, we're trying to work with reasonable goals here and not set ourselves up for failure.** Instead of trying to get twenty minutes done, try for five. Or two. Or just put one single thing away. Start small. Start *really* small. Start as small as you need. It's OK. The most important thing is just to do something, anything. It doesn't matter what it is or how insignificant it seems. You can do this.

MINI-CHALLENGE

- If you're in bed or on the couch, look at the surface nearest to you. It's likely a nightstand or coffee table. Set a timer for five minutes. Clear off as much of that surface as you can before the timer goes off. You can get right back in bed when you're done.

Try to do something—anything, really—that allows you to interact positively with your home every day. Whether that's cleaning, organizing, or even just displaying something that makes you happy, aim for getting one thing done every day that makes you feel better about where you live. If you have something happening every day that makes you feel overall more positive toward your home, it won't seem so hopeless while you're in the middle of what feels like nothing but negativity or apathy.

And never underestimate the importance of even just a little bit of progress. One of the worst things, among an almost infinite number of shitty things, about depression is that it makes you feel hopeless and worthless and like you can't do anything at all, let alone anything right. Setting yourself up for even the smallest positive accomplishment is so huge. You have this one small thing to point to as evidence that you aren't, in fact, worthless or hopeless. So what if it doesn't happen organically? The deck is already stacked against you here. You're not cheating; you're setting yourself up for a win, no matter how tiny it is. Clearing off your nightstand is a pretty big deal when you're depressed. Washing the dishes is practically like winning an Olympic gold medal. Why not give yourself a chance for one little positive emotion like pride or self-assurance when you otherwise feel kind of like shit?

MINI-CHALLENGE

- Gather up all the dirty dishes and bring them to the kitchen. Stop up the sink, fill it with hot soapy water, and let the dishes soak.

Cleaning your house is not going to cure your depression, but there's a good chance it'll help you feel a little less hopeless and desperate if you can look around and see that you're not surrounded by filth. It'll definitely help things seem a little less bleak. And when you're finally past this depressive episode, which you will be at some point, you'll have set yourself up in a better place to be a little less overwhelmed with all the stuff you need to do when you're feeling better.

There's a lot of talk about self-care during depressive episodes, but it can be really helpful to take care of Future You just as much as Present You. Seeing what's happened while you were in the middle of a bad time can be hard, making you feel ashamed of how bad things got all around you while your brain was screwing with you. By doing even just the smallest bit to keep things kind of in order, not only are you giving yourself something to focus on in the moment, you're also making things a little easier for yourself once you're out of that moment, however long it lasts.

In this process, it's so important to be kind to yourself. You might not be able to stop the negative thoughts flying through your brain—but that's OK. Show yourself some kindness. Be forgiving of what you're going through. Don't be too hard on yourself. A lot of this is out of your control, so take control over what you can and understand that the rest is going to happen, and it's going to suck, but you will get through it.

MINI-CHALLENGE

- Take a shower and change your clothes. Put the dirty clothes into the hamper.

ANXIETY

For many people, cleaning and organizing can be major anxiety triggers. Lots of people experience some form of anxiety about housekeeping, but when you live with a mental illness, this can be exacerbated many times over. Anxiety can spiral out of control when it's feeding on thoughts concerning a messy home. Whether it's about getting started, finishing up, or doing things "right," cleaning anxiety is a very real, very present thing.

If you find your anxiety is triggered by cleaning, try narrowing your focus a little bit. When you look at the big picture, it can be distressing to try to process everything involved in fixing it. It might be helpful to look at the situation one little section at a time. Limiting the scope of what you're going to deal with can help lower the chance of your anxiety being set off. Clear boundaries and definite beginning and ending points can help add some necessary structure.

Taking breaks is critical if you're dealing with anxiety that's triggered or made worse by cleaning. Periodically stopping is important because, in the midst of an anxiety episode, it can be very easy to keep going without pause and work yourself up even more. If you don't enforce taking breaks, you might soon find yourself marathoning, which is a good way to lose control.

By giving yourself definite boundaries, you can keep from feeling like you need to keep going until it's completely done. Tell yourself you're only going to do two or three 20/10s and then stop. You have a predetermined end in sight, so there's no need to feel guilt if everything isn't done when you stop. Hold yourself to these limits. Quit when you planned to. You're not going to be able to get to everything at once, and you shouldn't. So give yourself permission to stop, and let yourself enjoy the accomplishment of finishing what you did, even if it wasn't as much as you'd have liked.

- Set a timer for five minutes. Gather up as much trash as you can find and throw it away (or recycle where applicable) before the timer goes off.

Sometimes, making drastic changes in your living space can actually induce anxiety, and this includes going from messy to clean. You're removing a certain level of comfort and familiarity, and that can be disconcerting. Check in with yourself as you clean up. See if you can figure out how you're feeling when you look at an area you've just worked on. If you feel relieved or proud, it's probably fine to keep going. If you're anxious or upset, stop. Give yourself time to get used to the changes before you move on to the next thing. Anxiety can be very unpredictable, so if you feel yourself getting triggered, take a break, then maybe move on to something else. You can always come back to what you were doing.

CHILDHOOD CLEANING TRAUMA

For people who were raised in environments with unhealthy relationships to cleaning, cleaning can trigger anxiety, fear, depression, or panic. If you have a parent who was a hoarder, or you were raised in a household where cleaning was used as punishment, or you were disciplined for not cleaning properly or well enough, you may have some pretty negative mental stuff associated with cleaning.

If this is the case for you, first try to figure out where your negative associations with cleaning come from. If you can isolate that, you have a much better chance of figuring out how to work with it. If, for example, you were punished for not cleaning "correctly," or if cleaning was used as a punishment, institute a reward system for yourself with stuff you truly love. Washed the dishes? Go buy yourself a fancy coffee! Put your clothes away? Play to the next level in your video game. Whatever it takes to begin realizing that cleaning doesn't have to go hand in hand with negativity.

Children of hoarders face a particular set of challenges. Growing up in a home with a hoarder can lead to any number of psychological and physical problems, as well as the added challenge of trying to rebuild a healthy relationship with cleaning once you're out of the family home. Often, children of hoarders haven't developed the skills and routines associated with housekeeping that others learn in childhood. They may be lacking a context for when it's appropriate to keep things and when to throw them out. Although the children themselves may not grow up to be hoarders (although that certainly happens), hoarder parents may have passed on their emotional attachment to items, making it difficult for the kids—and the adults they become—to develop their own routines and standards.

It's also not uncommon for children of hoarders to grow up with extremely high standards of housekeeping. An early lifetime without any control over your living environment, surrounded by mess and clutter and often getting physically ill due to living conditions, can prompt you to want to exercise as much control as possible over your home and possessions. It's a good idea for children of hoarders to consider finding resources, whether online or in person, to help them deal with the psychological effects of growing up in a hoarding environment. (See the list of resources in the back of this book for a starting point.)

The Messy-House Cycle

One of the toughest concepts for people to wrap their heads around when it comes to housekeeping and cleaning is the fact that it's a never-ending cycle. Cleaning, by its very nature, is never actually finished. That's probably the most aggravating thing about it, and that's why most people can't stand doing it. You're never done. How annoying is that? So we rebel against it or ignore it entirely, because why on earth would we bother doing all that work, just to have to turn around and do it all over again in a few days or next week or next month? It's incredibly frustrating and makes the whole process seem pointless. And yeah, any task that needs to be repeated over and over really is a pain in the ass, because you never ever feel like you're finished. Hard truth time: You feel that way because you really *are* never finished. If you're looking at cleaning and housekeeping as an activity with an ultimate finish line, it's always going to result in a big *F* for *failure* in your mind. There's no way around it.

So before we get too far into the process of learning or relearning how to clean our homes, we need to make peace with the fact that it is indeed a cycle. There is no real "end." The point of figuring out a system for cleaning that works for you isn't to end that cycle, but to figure out which parts of the cycle you have control over and how to work with them in a way that results in a clean, comfortable home with the least amount of stress and frustration on your part. A lot of this will have to do with how long your particular cycle is: **How long do you let go by in between the individual steps of dealing with any particular part of your home?** This will determine how much time in total you're spending on that task and what the environment is like in between the times you're dealing with it. If your cycle for dishes is a week between using a dish and washing it, well, that's going to be a major contributing factor to your mess. If your cycle for dishes is once or twice a day, every day, you're going to find that you're actually spending less time doing them and also that everything is a hell of a lot cleaner in the time in between.

The shorter the cycle for any particular task, the less time you're going to take overall to do it. Sure, you're going to be revisiting the same thing more frequently, but by doing so, you're going to be spending a much shorter time doing it in general. Consider the difference between filing, recycling, or shredding one day's worth of mail (maybe five or ten pieces total?) in a minute or two, versus having to deal with several months' worth of mail, which can take the better part of a day. Not to mention that when you're spending a few hours or most of a day dealing with something, you're way more likely to get frustrated and disgruntled with it, whereas when you're just dealing with something for a few moments, it doesn't really have the chance to affect you at that level. So you just might find that when you start doing household tasks more often, you'll be less angry about them overall because you aren't spending huge amounts of time doing them.

Let's take a look at the cycle as a whole. As you live your life in your home, you use items and interact with your environment. That results in things getting messy and dirty, and then everything needs to get cleaned up. And you keep living your life, so the use/mess-up/clean cycle is ongoing and needs to happen again and again. People really seem to get stuck on that repetition part, and it's where most people who have difficulty cleaning get in trouble and give up. A lot of people seem to think that if they clean something once, they're done forever and that thing never needs to be cleaned again. Well, you can see how that might lead to feeling a little bit defeated when tomorrow or next week or next month comes around and that thing has been used once more and needs to be dealt with again.

The positive thing about this cycle without an end, though, is that there is always an opportunity for you to do better, do more, do it again, do it right, or even do it at all. There's no such thing as "failure" in this endeavor, because it is ongoing and continuous, so there's no end point at which you have to admit you failed. If you don't do what you hoped to accomplish today, you're still going to have the chance to do it tomorrow. Or next week. You can't fail at something cyclical like this. You may have times when you fall short of your expectations, but then you can try again and get it right. Or even just closer to right. There will be days when you don't do anything at all, and that sure feels like a failure, but then you'll tackle a big project or really get the rhythm of something like laundry or dishes, and you'll feel like a tremendous success. So stop looking at taking care of your home as a pass/fail situation and start to accept it as a constant chance to do better every day than you did the day before.

Mental health and housekeeping are often more closely linked than we realize. By understanding how cleaning and our mental health affect each other, we can interrupt the cycle that so often leaves us surrounded by chaos in a home we don't love. By developing coping mechanisms to lean on when our mental health is letting us down, we have the chance to come out on the other side a little bit better, and sometimes that's enough to make a difference.

THE PERFECTIONIST'S PARADOX

Perfectionism is a tricky concept when it comes to housekeeping. A lot of people use the fact that they're self-identified "perfectionists" as the main reason they can't keep a clean and organized home. Have you ever thought, "If I can't do it right, why bother doing it at all?" Or, "If I can't finish, it's pointless to even start"? It's a pretty common way to look at things, but it's kind of bullshit. Perfectionism is a double-edged sword. It's great to want to do everything exactly right, but it can also create a mindset in which you never start anything because you know you won't be able to do it perfectly. And more often than not, what we claim to be perfectionism is really just a bunch of other stuff like avoidance, feelings of inadequacy, impossible expectations, and so much more.

Perfectionism tends to work as a convenient excuse to explain why you're letting your mess linger. After all, if you don't start, you can't finish in a way that doesn't jibe with your perfectionist standards. That's incredibly convenient, because you've just put yourself in a situation where your "impossibly high standards" are giving you a handy excuse to keep on doing nothing at all. And while it's not unreasonable that your standards are, in fact, that high, it's also quite possible that those high standards stem from good old-fashioned avoidance.

There's a fair amount of contradiction in proclaiming that we can't stand for anything to be less than absolutely perfect while we're surrounded by an unholy mess of our own creation. While we're so proud of ourselves for having impossibly high standards, everything's going to absolute shit all around us. Saying you won't be satisfied until your home looks like a sparkling, pristine magazine photo means very little when your dirty clothes are littering the floor and you haven't emptied the dish drainer in weeks. This is the perfectionist's paradox when it comes to housework: Even though starting a load of laundry or putting the clean dishes away doesn't mean your home will be picture-perfect right away, it'll definitely be nicer than it is right now—but nicer isn't good enough, so you do nothing. It's weird to look at a messy home and think, "Oh yeah, a perfectionist definitely lives here." But it's so common! The good news is that perfectionism can be unlearned.

Perfectionists tend to be really hard on themselves in a lot of different ways. Rather than being constantly self-congratulatory for accomplishing so much so well, people who identify as perfectionists generally go through life feeling disappointed in themselves because nothing they do measures up to their own expectations. And perfectionism can come from a lot of places. Sometimes, it's entirely internal and self-imposed. Other times, it's imposed on us by people who tell us our best efforts aren't good enough, or make us feel as though no matter what we do, it's wrong. And it can come from people we don't even know. Those unattainable magazine spreads, those smug, aspirational lifestyle blogs—all of that can make us feel like a perfect result is the only option. It's not. Not at all. And you aren't doing yourself any favors by buying into it.

If you're hoping to change your perfectionist ways, it's worth examining why your standards are so high. Were you raised in an environment with people who didn't accept your best efforts unless those efforts resulted in excellence? Do you come from (or currently live in) an environment in which you feel like nothing you attempt is good enough, regardless of results? Were you praised during your formative years for being exemplary, and now you feel like you *have* to be immediately great at everything you try or else you'll let people (including yourself) down? Whether your drive for perfection is internal or placed on you by the expectations of others, it's worthwhile to try to figure out why you feel the way you do and how you can begin to overcome it.

"But why should I try to overcome it?" you may ask. Being a perfectionist seems pretty awesome, doesn't it? I mean, you want everything you do to be correctly done and absolutely perfect. What could possibly be wrong with that? Well, a lot, really. By saying nothing but 100 percent is good enough, what do you do when 100 percent isn't possible? Most likely, you do nothing. As we've established, even a small amount of progress is preferable to not getting started at all. Life doesn't exist at only 0 percent and 100 percent. There's a whole continuum of stages along the way, all of which mean you've progressed beyond

0 percent and are well on your way to 100 percent. But don't underestimate the importance of all of those other stages. You need them. They're necessary and important, even if your goal takes a little bit longer to achieve.

For your own sake, try to let go of this ideal of perfectionism. It's holding you back in ways you probably can't even see. Not only are you holding yourself to difficult (or potentially impossible) standards, you're giving yourself the OK to just avoid the problem entirely. Start trying to embrace small amounts of progress. Do a 20/10 or two and take a good critical look when you're done. No, it's not perfect, but is it better than when you started? If so, try to realize that any small improvement is more attainable and therefore more important than a perfect result on the first try. Doing something is always better than doing nothing. Even if you can't finish completely, you can at least get started and find yourself having made some progress rather than none at all.

This doesn't mean you have to stop deriving satisfaction from a job well done. It just means **you may need to redefine what a job well done really is.** If, in the past, you've been dissatisfied or unhappy with your progress until a project is complete, try giving yourself permission to stop partway through and take pride in what you've managed to do up to that point. Stopping before you normally would is great because it allows you to see that something exists between "haven't started" and "completely done," and that whatever effort you've put forth is valuable and worth celebrating. Forcing yourself to stop before the task is completed can be stressful and a little anxiety-inducing, so this is one of those times to reward yourself! If you do two or three 20/10s where you would normally do a full-day marathon, give yourself a treat to congratulate yourself on shaking up your way of thinking a little bit.

While you're at it, check in with your feelings and reactions during this process. If you really can't shrug off feeling disappointed or feeling like a failure, try giving yourself a smaller task that can be completed fully in a short period of time. That small victory of a fully completed job might be just enough to get you through that wave of negativity and closer to a sense of accomplishment. Or try taking "before" and "after" pictures. It's hard to argue with indisputable physical proof that you have made a noticeable (and documented) improvement in your surroundings. Try to recognize that a lot of the judgment you're feeling at this point originates internally. We are, for better or worse, our own worst critics, but there's no reason we can't also be our own biggest cheerleaders. Self-perception, when you get right down to it, is really the most important view of ourselves, so be as kind to yourself in your own mind as you'd want everyone else to be to you out loud.

Overcoming actual or perceived perfectionism can be tricky. It's difficult to give yourself permission to do something imperfectly or incompletely. What's important to keep in mind is that perfection is an impossible ideal. Even if you get your home perfectly clean and organized and gorgeous, you still live in it. You need to remember that no matter how well, how thoroughly, how perfectly you clean, it's going to get messy again, and it's going to do so pretty quickly. It's too easy to see this as a failure on your part, when it's absolutely not. If it were possible to clean something so thoroughly that it stayed clean forever, no one would ever need to read a book like this. Hundreds of websites and magazines would cease to exist, and messes would be a distant memory. Obviously, that's not the case. Shit gets messy over and over again, and it needs to be cleaned over and over again. Embrace the imperfect, knowing that you'll have plenty of chances to do it over and get it right (or close to right, even). Reframe your thinking to acknowledge that **the value in a task isn't necessarily in its completion, but in the very undertaking of it,** no matter how far you get.

As important as letting go of the idea of perfectionism is letting go of perfectionism as part of your identity. When you think that perfectionism is a defining part of who you are, it's that much harder to overcome the expectations you put on yourself as a result. Perfectionism isn't who you are; it's something you do. It's a behavior, a mindset, not a fundamental part of your personality. You can let go of perfectionism without sacrificing who you are as a person. It might be difficult, moving on, to accept something less than the flawless execution of a task, but if you can learn to derive the same feeling of accomplishment from simply doing, rather than doing perfectly, you'll probably be better off. (Not to mention that things will actually start getting done.)

If you're setting unattainable goals for yourself, not accepting anything less than a perfect result, you're not being fair to yourself. You're setting yourself up for failure at every juncture, and being ruled by catastrophic thinking ("If my house isn't spotless, I'll die of embarrassment"). Striving for perfection, like any other source of anxiety, is something that's not entirely within your control, but you can limit or mitigate the black-and-white thinking that dictates perfectionist tendencies. **Let go of "perfect" and embrace "good enough."** Engage in realistic thinking. What's the worst-case scenario if the task is imperfectly done? Is having a somewhat cleaner living environment better than whatever it is right now? How much imperfection can you comfortably live with? Once you can answer these questions and figure out how to move forward with progress, no matter how imperfect, you'll be happier in general as well as happier with your home and the mess within it.

2

UNFUCKING YOUR OWN HABITAT

Building Habits

More Stuff Than Storage

Cleaning Basics

Small Spaces

BUILDING HABITS

It's really easy to decide you're going to make broad, sweeping changes to your life and the way you interact with your stuff. It's a hell of a lot harder to actually do it. The larger the change you're hoping to make, the harder it is to make it. Expecting to just wake up one morning with a clean, organized home and the ability to keep it that way is just setting yourself up for all kinds of disappointment. There's a reason that all of your past attempts haven't been successful: **You can't change everything all at once, and you shouldn't try to.**

One of the main reasons so many of us fail to maintain our homes even if we manage to get them clean in the first place is because we haven't done anything to change our habits. Marathon cleaning is not a habit; it's a one-time deal, an intermittent and unpredictable binge with nothing to follow it up. In between marathon sessions, you aren't doing anything to prevent yourself from needing to do another one down the road. The only way we can be successful in not just getting but *keeping* our homes clean is by changing our daily habits, both large and small. Actually, the small changes are the most important. They require the least amount of time investment and the least amount of thought, but over time, those small habits are going to be what make the biggest difference overall.

Completely restructuring the way you think about and approach cleaning is a massive undertaking, and not everyone can do it easily. What you can do, though, is flip a series of tiny switches in your behavior that add up to noticeable, sustainable changes. Once these habits are second nature to you, you'll find your overall mess is reduced by a lot, and the amount of time you spend dealing with it will drastically decrease, too. These changes are useful because each one is relatively small, and small changes are so much easier to make and maintain than big ones. So by incorporating each of these small habits into your everyday life, you'll be making a big difference without having to completely change your mindset, and because of that, you'll be in a much better position to keep up with things where you may have failed to do so before.

DO A LITTLE BIT EVERY DAY

This ties back to 20/10s and incremental progress: By doing something, anything, every day, you avoid the need for a massive cleaning session once a month or once a year or just once ever—whatever it is you've been doing. If you're doing even a small amount of work on a daily basis, you not only catch up with the mess you've made that day but also help to get yourself a little bit ahead of the curve by making a dent in your baseline mess. Over time, you'll find that with just one twenty-minute session on the days you "don't have time," you can start in on the bigger projects that have been plaguing the landscape of your home for longer than you can remember.

As far as not having the time, especially during the week when you're working or at school or trying to keep up with everyone in your household and the million things you're each involved in, well, I'm pretty sure we all manage to find twenty minutes to catch up on Facebook or to see what's on Netflix. So it's not that we don't have time; it's just that we're choosing to prioritize the little bits of time we do have differently.

USE YOUR LEISURE TIME WISELY

About that Netflix thing. We're extremely lucky to live in a technologically advanced, highly mobile era, but these privileges can be an incredibly effective distraction, allowing us to lose hours at a time to something that's caught our interest. Do something while you're catching up on your series. Fold clothes and pair up all of your socks. Bring the laptop into the kitchen and clear off a counter. Find a twenty-minute podcast you like and use it as a soundtrack while you catch up on dishes. You don't have to stop your life in order to clean; you can integrate a little bit of housework into what you're already doing.

When you're trying to incorporate a small cleaning session into each day, you may find it helpful to get your twenty minutes in as soon as you get home, before you change out of your outside clothes and while you're still in a "working" mindset. Once your mind transitions to "I'm home, I'm relaxed, and I'm going to be living on the couch in my underwear until I go to bed," it's really difficult to transition back into "Maybe I should load the dishwasher." Figure out when you're likely to be able to squeak a tiny bit of productivity out of your tired self, and make it a point to do something when you can.

USE YOUR WAITING TIME EFFICIENTLY

We all have short spans of time during our day when we're stuck waiting for something else to finish before we can move on to the next thing. Learning how to use that time instead of letting it pass is a great habit to get into. While your coffee is brewing in the morning, unload the dishwasher from last night. Once you put dinner on to simmer or bake, wash all of your prep dishes so there's less to do later. Does your shower take a while to heat up? Use that dead time (and a sponge soaked with the not-hot-enough water) to wipe down the bathroom counters. While the microwave is going, wash a few dishes. Every little bit helps, and it's time that you'd just be wasting by staring off into space anyway. Might as well be productive, right?

There are a million little things we can do while we're waiting on other things. What's great about almost all of them is that they're really easy, low-investment, low-commitment things that still make a big difference. Once you start doing this, you'll find yourself surprised by how little time it actually takes to do things compared to how much time you're assuming it will. Get into the habit of not staying idle while life annoyingly takes time to happen around you.

PUT IT AWAY, NOT DOWN

One of the most effective habits for keeping our chaos under control is *putting things away where they belong* instead of just setting them down. Every time you set empty packaging on the counter instead of putting it in the recycling bin, every time you kick your shoes off and leave them wherever they land instead of sticking them back in the closet, every time you return from a shopping trip and set the bags on the counter instead of putting the items away, you're making the mess worse. By being mindful about where items end up, you can keep the chaos from escalating. Once you have a clean surface, room, or home, the very act of simply returning things to their proper place will make more of a difference than almost anything else. Don't have a home for all your things? You need one! Go straight to "More Stuff than Storage" on page TK. 70

Go straight to "More Stuff than Storage" on page TK. 70

MINI-CHALLENGE

- **Look around. Find ten things that aren't where they belong. Put them away.**

Once you start becoming aware of where you're putting things, you'll notice that it's really not as much work as you think to put things away instead of setting them down wherever. The best part about changing this particular habit is that the better you become at it, the less you have to clean up later on. It's basically a gift from Right Now You to Future You. You're never going to look back and say, "Boy, I'm glad I just left all that stuff I bought the other day out on the counter so I'd have to deal with it later or pretend it doesn't exist." Future You is going to resent the hell out of Right Now You for not putting that shit away when you got home. But how awesome is it to look at a previously cleaned countertop that's *still* clean because you're not using it as a way station for every bit of crap that you bring through the door? A little bit of effort in the present is going to save you a ton of time in the future.

MAKE YOUR BED

I can hear you whining from here, seriously. I know you don't want to make your bed. I know you don't see the point. I've heard every excuse and rationalization imaginable for not making your bed (and some that I definitely had never imagined). But a messy bed makes a room look messier, and a made bed brings a focal point of cleanliness and order, making even a messy room look a little bit better. It's also a small but obvious form of control over your environment. Unmade beds are agents of entropy; they're only going to get worse. First the bedding is in disarray. Then laundry starts to pile up on it. Then there's so much other stuff on it that there's no room to sleep unless you toss everything on the floor. Sometime later, you realize you can't remember when you last washed your sheets. Taking a minute to make your bed immediately snaps some order into the chaos. It's also a great place to start if you aren't ready to tackle anything more complex. It's one step, one tiny thing you do in the morning, and then you're done.

Bed-Making 101

Making your bed doesn't have to be a complicated production. Just pull the sheets up, straighten the blankets, and put the pillows back where they belong. If you're someone who believes your bed needs to "breathe" (although you do much more in the war against dust mites by washing your sheets on a regular basis and giving your mattress a semiregular vacuuming, some people are really, *really* into the idea that beds need to breathe), fold your sheets and blankets down neatly by the foot of the bed and arrange your pillows.

Oh, and I can just hear some of you now: "Why should I make my bed? I'm just going to mess it up later anyway." Well, smartasses, you wash your dishes even though you're going to use them later. You hang your clothes up even though you're going to wear them later. You throw your trash away even though you're going to make more later. The continued use of an item doesn't mean you never have to clean or maintain it. Just make your damn bed. You'll be surprised at how much cleaner your bedroom looks from that one thing.

There's this fundamental resistance that people have to making their beds, which comes from a whole lot of different places. Most often, it's because you were made to do it as a child, and refusal to do it as an adult is a way of reclaiming some control over your environment. And that's totally fine! It's human nature to rebel against structure that has been imposed upon us, especially in our younger years when we had little to no power of our own. If that's the case, it may be difficult to come back around to choosing to make your own bed, but perhaps with time, you'll see the benefit and decide to do it.

KEEP YOUR FLAT SURFACES CLEAR

This is as much psychological as anything else. Flat surfaces like counters, tables, dressers, nightstands, etc., tend to accumulate a lot of crap. When they're all piled up with stuff, visually, they're messy, they're overwhelming, they make everything look bad, and the whole thing makes you feel like conquering your mess is hopeless. By keeping the most visible flat surfaces clear on a daily basis, you'll have tangible proof that your cleaning and organizing efforts do, in fact, make a difference.

There are practical benefits, too! Most messes tend to build up on flat surfaces, so when you clear them off, you're not just playing mind games with yourself; you're actually tackling a fairly significant portion of your overall mess. Even if you can't clean everything, you can still get one table or counter completely clear and keep it that way with minimal effort every day, and that one surface is going to go a long way toward a cleaner home in general.

Surface Cleaning 101

Pick a surface that you see multiple times a day that tends to accumulate clutter, devote one or two (or five; no judgment here) 20/10s to clearing it off completely, and then take five minutes or so every day to reset it back to clean. If your kitchen counter always ends up a mess of shopping bags, junk mail, and random things you just drop there because it's easier, make that your focus. If your nightstand is so crowded that you can't fit your phone on it overnight to charge, that might be a good place to start. Pick somewhere highly visible that tends to amass more crap than seems possible, and clear it off. Make sure you aren't just relocating the mess somewhere else; find a logical home for each item and put it away. If you make this into a daily habit, stuff won't have the chance to turn your flat surfaces into giant, unmanageable disaster zones.

UNFUCK TOMORROW MORNING

Let's face it, mornings are chaos. We wait until the last possible minute to wake up, get ready for the day half-asleep, usually forget something critical in our mad rush, and fly out the door basically unprepared for the day ahead because we've just completely run out of time to get ready. None of us are at our best when we're bleary-eyed and trying not to be late. In keeping with our theme of "a little bit of effort now saves you a lot of work later," try setting up a nightly routine that makes the next morning go a little more smoothly. I know, I know; this just reeks of your mom yelling at you to lay out your outfit the night before school, but work with me a little bit here. It makes sense.

Think realistically about what trips you up in the morning. Do you lose time trying to find matching shoes or your keys? Is trying to throw together a last-minute lunch costing you time (or money in takeout, because let's face it, that's way easier)? Do you forget to take your meds only to realize it when you're on the road and your pills are at home, forgotten? Get all that shit together the night before and make your morning that much easier. **Doing twenty minutes' worth of work before bed can save you endless aggravation in the morning.** Remember, Future You will appreciate whatever Right Now You manages to do to make life a little easier.

HOW TO UNFUCK TOMORROW MORNING . . . TONIGHT!

- **Wash the dishes in your sink.**
- **Get your outfit for tomorrow together, including accessories.**
- **Set up coffee/tea/breakfast.**

- **Make your lunch.**

- **Put your keys somewhere obvious.**

- **Take your medication/set out your meds for the morning.**

- **Charge your electronics.**

- **Pour a little cleaner in the toilet bowl (if you don't have pets or children or sleepwalking adults).**

- **Set your alarm.**

- **Go to bed at a reasonable hour.**

TRASH GOES IN THE TRASH CAN

Seems pretty basic, right? Well, take a look around and see how many dryer sheets, pieces of food packaging, supermarket flyers, napkins, shopping bags, and other assorted pieces of trash you have sitting around. It's a fact of human nature: Sometimes the trash doesn't make it to the trash can. (Same goes for recycling.) While this is certainly an extension of "put it away, not down," it also requires a little bit of self-awareness. What trash are you creating, and what do you do with it once you create it? Packaging is a common culprit here. You buy something new, take it out of the packaging, and get right to using it. Meanwhile, the empty packaging is sitting on the counter where you left it, forgotten forever (or at least until your next big cleanup). Just a few extra seconds and a couple more steps can solve that problem.

If you don't have some kind of trash receptacle in every room, get one. Throwing your trash away is a lot easier when it doesn't require a special trip. Make sure your recycling bin is accessible, too. It's not worth it to invest in some kind of complex sorting system if it's too far away or so inconvenient to get to that you'll never use it. The solution can be as simple as another trash can, designated just for recycling, stored right next to your existing trash can. Don't make it more complicated than it needs to be. Of course, part of this habit is taking the trash and recycling out of your house on a regular basis. If you have a designated trash pickup day, make sure you're keeping up with it. If not, assign yourself a day when you take all the garbage and recyclables wherever they need to go once they leave your home.

DO THE DISHES EVERY DAY

Listen, it's just a fact that dirty dishes multiply infinitely until they fill up every square inch of available space in your home. The longer you leave them, the more they breed, until the best option to deal with them seems to be lighting a match and hoping a nice cleansing fire will make them go away. But it doesn't have to be this way. If you can manage to incorporate doing your dishes into your daily routine, you'll only need to invest a few minutes at a time in dealing with them, rather than having to set aside the better part of an afternoon. And best of all? No fire involved.

Dishes are probably the most-hated household chore in existence, and they also tend to be some of the worst contributors to a mess. Those two things are not a coincidence; dishes are such a problem because we hate dealing with them. But if you keep up with your dishes every single day rather than letting them sit and fester, they become just a tiny annoyance rather than an undefeatable enemy. Try to get into the habit of dealing with your dishes immediately after using them. If doing the dishes is just as much a part of mealtime as food preparation and eating, you'll soon find that the dish problem isn't that much of a problem after all.

WASH, DRY, AND PUT IT AWAY, GODDAMMIT

Laundry and dishes have three steps, everyone. It's not done until it's put away.

Be honest: How much laundry do you have sitting around where it doesn't belong? Clean clothes languishing in laundry baskets, finished loads sitting in the dryer? And let's not forget the ever-present **floordrobe.** Your floor (or chair, bed, desk) is not the best place to keep your clothes. I bet you have dressers and/or closets and such designed especially to deal with all of those clothes! The trouble is, they're not going to do you any good unless you use them. First things first, though: You can't put things away if everything doesn't have a home. So make sure you have enough storage for your stuff, and if not, it's time to look into less stuff or more storage. (Less stuff is almost always the better and easier answer.) Once you have adequate storage, you actually need to use it. (See "More Stuff than Storage" on page TK for some UfYH-approved guidelines.)

Putting your clothes away saves you from doing a ton of laundry, too, because sometimes you just scoop stuff up and wash it, even if you're not sure it's actually dirty. (You know you do—it's easier than taking a couple of extra seconds to figure out whether or not you can wear it again). Make sure all of your laundry has a place, so that when you do a load or two, putting it away isn't a major feat of engineering and organization. Once you have a home for everything, the only reason for leaving clean clothes all over the place is your own unwillingness to take a few extra minutes to put them away. It's OK. We've all been there, but now we're trying to get past it. Make it a habit to get clean clothes to where they belong immediately after everything is dry, rather than leaving things neglected in the dryer, in the laundry basket, or on the drying rack . . . or on the floor.

MINI-CHALLENGE

- **Do you have laundry that needs to be put away? Go put ten items away. Maybe even empty a whole laundry basket.**

As far as dishes go, washing them is great, but it's a big pain-in-the-ass process that none of us enjoys. It's gross and your hands get all wet and you have to stand up for a long time and it's just tedious. If you're facing a sink full of dirty dishes, there's very little in the world that's less appealing than having to take the time to wash them and leave them to dry. Including the additional step of putting them away makes the whole process seem even crappier. Even if you're lucky enough to have a dishwasher, you still need to load it and run it, which is kind of annoying, too. So I understand the inclination to want to stand back and celebrate once you've gotten the damn things washed; really, I do. But you aren't done until they're put away. Running the dishwasher is all well and good, but if your sink is accumulating a mountain of dirty dishes because your clean ones are still camped out in the dishwasher, well, your dish system isn't working so well. Put them away. Same rules apply if you hand wash and use a drying rack. Either put them away as soon as they're dry, or help the process along by grabbing a dish towel and drying them right away.

The habit of "put it away, goddammit" is a fairly advanced one because it adds time to an already unpleasant process, and it requires expending extra effort after you've already worked pretty hard on getting the stuff clean and dry. It takes a little longer to incorporate into your everyday routine. But once you've gotten into the habit of putting your dishes and laundry away, you'll find yourself so much further ahead of the game than you started out.

DEAL WITH YOUR INVISIBLE CORNERS

After you've been living somewhere for a significant amount of time, you start to accumulate things in spaces I refer to as "invisible corners." Invisible corners are those areas that have become dumping grounds for random crap for so long that you fail to really register them when you look around. Maybe it's a pile of unshredded mail and random electronic accessories stashed under an end table, or a stack of unpacked boxes in a little-used closet, or that jumble of daily detritus that permanently lives on the kitchen counter. Whatever and wherever your particular collections of stuff are, chances are they've been there long enough that you barely see them anymore, even when they're right in your way day in and day out.

Invisible corners can contribute to the overall mess in a way that you might not realize. After spending a bunch of time doing your regular maintenance cleaning, you may find that your space still doesn't feel clean for some reason. That might be due to an invisible corner or two that's leading to an overall feeling of disarray. These spots, for some reason, have proven to be convenient or easy places to stash things you aren't dealing with, so they become a jumble of miscellaneous stuff that just grows and grows over time, unnoticed and unaddressed.

To find your invisible corners, it might be necessary to employ some "before" pictures or even another set of eyes. You might be registering these areas in the same way you register your walls or furniture: not at all. You know they're there, but they never sink in as something you actually need to deal with. So consider taking a 360-degree set of pictures and really looking at them to see what spots you have that need to be dealt with. Or bring in a trusted friend or family member to take a look around and see what jumps out. A fresh set of eyes is sometimes all it takes to point out areas that are obvious to others but invisible to you.

<hr>

TACKLE AN INVISIBLE CORNER

- **Take a set of pictures of one main room in your home, making sure every part of the room is in at least one picture. Identify an invisible corner that needs to be cleaned up. Set a timer for twenty minutes and work on it, taking a ten-minute break afterward. Repeat with another 20/10 if needed until the area is all cleaned up.**

<hr>

Invisible corners can exist anywhere, large or small, hidden or exposed. You may have them in your refrigerator, in a closet, in the middle of the living room, in your front entryway, at the foot of your bed, anywhere. They can consist of just three or four items, or they can be stacks and stacks of boxes containing dozens of things each. Regardless of the size or scope of the invisible corner, it's not going to get any better unless you identify and disassemble it.

The great thing about invisible corners is that they generally don't take that long to deal with. They've grown and accumulated stuff over who knows how long, but they can almost always be managed in a few 20/10s. The difficult part is keeping them from reappearing. Something about those particular spots makes them prime dumping grounds for stuff, and you've already proven that you can ignore their existence on a daily basis. You may have success with rearranging things so that the spot is no longer able to accumulate stuff, or you may need to add it into your maintenance-cleaning routine. Whatever method you employ to deal with them, make sure your invisible corners aren't reappearing due to inattention.

TAKE PICTURES

Everyone loves a makeover, but the trouble with cleaning up your own mess is that sometimes when you're in the middle of it, it's really difficult to see any progress that you've made. Your brain is constantly updating its internal picture of what that space looks like, so you don't necessarily remember exactly how messy it was to begin with. Snapping a quick picture before you start and then at intervals throughout the cleaning process, and finally when you're finished, accomplishes several things. First, after working for a while, you're likely to feel like you haven't made any noticeable progress. **Having a clear "before" picture reminds you what it really looked like to start, and how far you've come.** It can also be helpful in pointing out hidden areas that need attention. By letting you look at the environment from outside, a good "before" picture can help you turn a critical eye to the area and see things you may not have noticed before.

Plus, once you're finished and the area is clean, you have visual proof of what you've accomplished, and also a reference to look at once things start getting messy again. When things start to accumulate and it all begins to feel hopeless, you can always refer back to your pictures to remind yourself that not only can you do it, but you *have* done it. Remind yourself that your home can be nice and clean, and that you have the ability to make it that way. Use your "after" pictures as a guide to help you remember what any particular area looks like when it's actually clean and to serve as a rough template for how to get that space back to neat and organized.

So before you tackle that closet from hell or prepare to do battle with the Crap That Ate the Dining Room Table, take a picture; then snap a few during the process, and take one when you're done. Your brain may not see the improvements you've made, but your camera sure as hell will. It's your objective eye that sees things much more clearly and accurately than the ones in your head when you're in the middle of everything. Fire up the camera; it's worth it.

MORE STUFF
THAN STORAGE

In a perfect world, cleaning and organizing coexist peacefully. In the real world, sometimes we're good at one but not the other, and sometimes we're just terrible at both. Ultimately, before you can begin to clean, you need to uncover enough surface area to actually *have* something to clean. This requires organizational skills. This also, however, is where so many people stall out and give up before they ever make any progress. In its own way, organization is more difficult than cleaning, because it's not always dictated by common sense, and it's often overwhelming and frustrating.

There's no shortage of books and articles and websites telling you how to organize your stuff. Most people try over and over again to get organized and end up falling short of success, only to turn around and try the same thing again . . . and again. Shockingly, it rarely works those times, either. So it's worthwhile to take a step back and look at why so many of these organizational tips and systems don't work for so many people, and try a new approach that does.

One of the main reasons we give up on trying to organize our stuff is, frankly, that it's a lot of effort. Not many of us have unlimited time and energy to devote to getting our mess under control. But—here's another way that 20/10s and working in small sections can come in handy. A full overhaul of, say, your closet can take hours or days, leaving you completely worn out at the end and unlikely to ever want to go through the whole process again. But when you give yourself small, attainable goals, you'll end up making far more progress in the long term, and not being so afraid of the upkeep. By tackling one drawer, shelf, or cabinet at a time, you're less likely to find yourself giving up, frustrated and surrounded by every item you own strewn about the floor with no idea what to do with any of them.

We're disorganized primarily because we have more stuff than storage. **There are two solutions: less stuff or more storage. Less stuff is almost always the better option.** You've probably seen all the "helpful tips" and "how to get organized" lists that tell you about cute, creative storage solutions to organize a whole lot of crap you probably don't need. Everything is much easier to organize when you don't have so much of it. Not to mention that storage is expensive, takes up a lot of room, and can be overwhelming to set up.

THE DARK SIDE OF MINIMALISM

"Less stuff" can be a bit of a trap, however. The recent obsession with "decluttering" has its downsides. The quest for minimalism can ultimately leave you feeling like a failure if you don't get rid of every single item you own and surround yourself with a sterile, Spartan environment. You should absolutely aim to reduce the number of items you have, especially if you have a lot of things that you don't use or don't love, but not to the point where you end up chucking everything you own. Perhaps more important is figuring out what you actually need, and learning how to work with that.

Let's face it, to function well in modern life, you need a certain amount of stuff. You don't necessarily need five of every item you own, but unless you're thinking of moving to a mountaintop and living only off the land, purging everything but your bed, one set of dishes, and a single change of clothes isn't much more helpful than keeping every item that crosses your path. **Compulsive decluttering and compulsive hoarding are opposite sides of the same coin; they both result in extreme behavior that dictates how you interact with the stuff around you.** Getting rid of everything you own is not healthier or any better to aspire to than never getting rid of anything at all, and yet we tend to view a minimalist home as something we should constantly be striving toward. More important than just chucking every one of your possessions is to find a good balance between utility and minimalism, a balance that allows you to take a critical look at the things you have, use, and need, and figure out what to keep, what to get rid of, and how to organize what's left.

While minimalism might seem like a noble goal, it's important to realize that it might be unattainable. If you're constantly questing to get rid of things, you may never be satisfied, because it's basically impossible to reduce your possessions to nothing. A better perspective, then, may be to look at what a realistic and attainable amount of stuff to have is. This amount is going to vary greatly from person to person and household to household, and there's no real "right" answer. Figuring out your minimum workable amount of stuff is tricky, and the process of deciding what stays and what goes isn't terribly straightforward. You need to consider an item's utility: Do you use it? How often? Do you have other items that have the same use? Consider its value—not just monetarily, but its value to you. Consider how you feel about it: Does its presence evoke any emotions in you, positive or negative? If something's very presence in your home stresses you out, why are you keeping it? All of these factors are important to weigh when you're examining your stuff and trying to decide what to keep and what to get rid of, and it's never as cut-and-dried as it seems like it should be.

Redefine minimalism to fit your own life. Don't get caught up in the trap of minimalism as it's presented in books, magazines, and websites. It's a nice, soothing aesthetic, but it's really not practical for most people. Reducing your number of possessions is a great goal; it'll make a huge difference in the level of mess in your home, and make everything easier to keep on top of. Just try not to get overwhelmed making your home look like carefully staged pictures of rooms that actual people never use.

And then there's the whole concept of "decluttering." How do you decide what is, in fact, unnecessary? Is it all of the things you own? Everything that's taking up space? Everything that's visible? Only the unnecessary stuff? By setting up this whole category apart from "cleaning" and "organizing," we're placing as much importance on throwing shit away as we do on every other aspect of keeping a house. And while getting rid of unwanted or extraneous stuff is a critical part of getting organized, people tend to think that once the "decluttering" phase is complete, their homes are magically tidy and organized forever. Getting to the point of having less stuff is important, but there's far more to getting a mess under control than just that.

Put your effort, instead, into making sure that all of the things you own have both a use and a place. If something has a use but no place, it's always going to seem in the way. And if something has a place but no use, it's taking up valuable storage space that might be better occupied by an item that has a useful value to you. Don't try to get rid of everything you own. You'll drive yourself to frustration just trying. And don't make the mistake of thinking that once you've pared down your stuff, you're done. You aren't. That's just one part of it; you still need to do a bunch more on a regular basis to keep things in order. It's a great start, and an important part of the process, but it's just one step of many.

Should it stay, or should it go?

When you're trying to decide what to keep and what to toss, you need to ask yourself some pertinent questions. For example:

- **WHEN WAS THE LAST TIME I USED THIS?** Sure, maybe that kitchen blowtorch seemed like a great idea at the time, but how many times have you actually made crème brûlée? And how long ago was that? If you can't remember when you last used it, you don't need to hang on to it.

- **AM I EVER GOING TO NEED THIS AGAIN?** Admit it, you looked hot in those bell-bottoms. But ask yourself, even if bell-bottoms come back in style, are you going to wear them, or is that a phase best left in the past forever? If an item's usefulness has passed, get rid of it.

- **AM I KEEPING THIS BECAUSE THERE'S A SMALL CHANCE I MIGHT NEED IT LATER?** So you've never been camping, but that camping kitchen set was just too cute to pass up. Sure, you can't sleep without your 800-thread-count sheets, and bugs of all kinds horrify you, but you might decide to rough it sometime, right? Be honest. You won't.

- **AM I HOLDING ON TO IT BECAUSE I FEEL GUILTY FOR SPENDING MONEY ON IT?** Deciding to get rid of something you parted with your hard-earned money for can be difficult. But keeping something indefinitely when you don't use it isn't going to get you your money back. Accept that the cash is gone, and aim to make your financial decisions a little more carefully next time.

GIFTS; OR, "JUST WHAT I NEEDED! MORE STUFF!"

When attempting to sort through possessions, many people get stuck on what to do with gifts. Gifts are tricky; they fall into a category of stuff that has a lot of emotion attached to it. Gifts inspire nostalgia, fondness, regret, even guilt. We so often feel guilty about getting rid of gifts that we end up hanging on to stuff that we never would have willingly brought into our homes in the first place. We feel like it's a betrayal of the giver to get rid of gifts, that somehow not keeping the things people give us is a reflection of our relationship with them. It's not.

Why does getting rid of gifts cause us so much stress? When we have items all wrapped up in emotions, we cease making decisions about them based on their own merits and allow our emotions to guide us. That's where we get into trouble. When inanimate items start taking on emotional importance, they become far more difficult to deal with in a logical, organized way. The gift itself doesn't feel anything; the emotions that are attached to it come a little bit from the giver and primarily from the recipient. So stop worrying that you're treating a gift badly by getting rid of it. You won't hurt its feelings, I promise. Because it doesn't have any.

You should look critically at gifts the same way you look at any other item you're trying to make a decision about—Do you use it? Do you love it? Is it necessary? Is it stressing you out? Why are you keeping it? The answers will usually jump right out at you. You don't use it; if you love it, it's only because of who gave it to you; it's unnecessary; its presence stresses you out; you're only keeping it because you feel guilty getting rid of it. With any other item, your course of action would be clear: Get rid of it. But the fact that it's a gift gives you pause. It shouldn't.

The real value of a gift is in the giving and receiving of it. The actual item itself is far less important. The crucial thing to remember is that once a gift is given, it belongs to you, and you're free to get rid of it whenever and however you please. It's incredibly rare that the giver of a gift will demand proof of its continued place in your home. (And if you think that might happen, have them over for dinner, show them their knickknack proudly displayed, and then send it on its way to the recycle bin once they've left.) The giver picked it out and gave it to you, you were (at least convincingly) pleased by it, and now the gift-giving interaction is done. It made them happy to give it, it made you happy to receive it, and now it's over. The thing is yours. Make it go away if you want it to go away. It doesn't make you a bad person or an ungrateful gift recipient if you don't hang on to a gift for all eternity.

HOW NOT TO GET RID OF YOUR STUFF

First and foremost, when you're getting rid of stuff, don't make it someone else's problem. It's really appealing to think that our discarded items will be useful, cherished items for other people, but that's not always true. Donating things is a great way to thin out your belongings, but make sure that what you're donating isn't something that you've just made someone else responsible for permanently getting rid of. Before donating anything, double-check with the organization you're donating to to make sure your items are in appropriate condition and that you're following the guidelines for donation. If something is broken, outdated, or no longer useful, you're really just passing the buck on ending its life cycle when you know good and well that it was time for it to get tossed or recycled.

Giving things to people you know is tricky, too. Many of your friends and family won't say no when you offer things to them, but it doesn't necessarily mean they want them. While it's appealing to think these people will love and treasure our secondhand belongings, most people already have more stuff than they know what to do with, and unloading more crap on them is hardly doing anyone a favor. So often, what we give to other people in the name of streamlining our belongings becomes a burden on the people we give those things to. Then they're in the position of having to evaluate and decide what to do with your castoffs. Don't do that to them. Think about the process you're going through right now. Do you really want to be responsible for putting another person through the same ordeal: sorting through a bunch of stuff and desperately trying to get rid of unwanted things? Your friends, family, and neighbors aren't convenient receptacles for your cast-offs. Don't treat them as if they are.

A better way to go about it is to ask people if there's anything they need (generally) or want (specifically). If your brother tells you he really needs a coffeepot and you've got a spare, that decision is easy. If your coworker has always coveted your laptop bag and you were trying to decide if it was worth hanging on to, that information might help you out. If your cousin has her eye on your favorite pair of shoes, it's perfectly fine to tell her those aren't up for grabs. (But hey, if you want to clear them out at some point in the future, you have a place to start!) Make considerate, informed decisions about giving your stuff away. Don't just transfer your problems to someone else because it's easier on you.

STORAGE

Once you've pared things down to items that are useful or necessary or that just make you happy, you need to figure out where the hell to put them. To do this effectively, you need to look at a few things:

- How often do you use it?
- Where do you use it?
- Do you have somewhere logical near where you use it to put it?
- Can you create somewhere logical to put it?

Ideally, your storage will allow you easy access to an item—so it's quick to grab and quick to put away—and be close to where you use it. Storing your heavy blender on a top shelf behind your pots and pans is going to make it hard to get to and a pain to put away when you make your daily smoothie. Infrequently used items can be stored in more inconvenient places, but your everyday items should live someplace where it's just as easy to put them away as it is to leave them out. The more convenient a storage space, the more likely you'll actually put things away rather than leaving them out to deal with at some mysterious point in the future.

Also keep in mind the realities of your life. If you're short, vertical storage up to the ceiling is going to be of limited use to you. You'd be better off exploring storage options that are accessible, like floor and under-furniture storage. If you have mobility issues, storage that requires you to climb a flight of stairs to retrieve something and again to put it away is best saved for those things that you won't need to get very often. If you have a cat who loves to climb, open cabinets are probably not the best idea, since all of your meals will be served with a side of Smokey's hair. What might seem like a perfect solution in theory might end up being completely incompatible with your life.

Some more things to keep in mind regarding storage:

- **KEEP IT CLOSED.** Open storage (shelves, cabinets without fronts, etc.) tends to look messy, no matter how well things are organized. If that's your only option, consider creating a uniform front using boxes or baskets, or closing off your storage with fabric or improvised doors. Open storage usually also requires more frequent dusting. Nobody wants that. Magazines and home blogs love depicting open storage, and it always seems to look great when they do it, but keep in mind that how things play out in real life is always very different than how they look in carefully staged photos.

- **MISMATCHED STORAGE CREATES VISUAL CHAOS.** A lot of the time, we end up with mismatched storage because, frankly, storage is really expensive (see below) and buying a matched set all at once isn't always possible. The cheapest option is usually pretty appealing, but just keep in mind that a piecemeal assortment of different storage can result in a messy finished look, no matter how much work went into the actual organization. Cheap is in no way bad; just make sure it's cheap that matches well enough to look put-together.

- **STORAGE IS EXPENSIVE.** Often very expensive. When you look at pictures of well-organized spaces with lots of great storage, those spaces usually have one thing in common: You can't afford them. And that sucks so much. A lot of the time, magazine spreads feature extravagant built-ins, closet systems, or well-constructed matching pieces, and for many people, that's just not an option. Since an elaborate storage system is out of reach for many of us, keep the amount of stuff that you have to a reasonable minimum; your storage needs will be far easier to deal with and far cheaper to implement.

- **ONLY STORE WHAT YOU NEED.** Don't store stuff you don't want, and don't create storage black holes. Random baskets and bins without a purpose are just asking to be catchalls for crap you should really be dealing with in a different way. Empty storage can be an appealing trap: somewhere you can throw stuff so you don't need to make any decisions about it and it's not out in the open. Don't do that, because you will at some point need to make a decision about the random assortment of crap that you tossed in those baskets and bins. Plus, you'll need to buy more of those pricey bins to keep it all in. Only store stuff that you've already decided to keep and use.

- **SMALL SPACES REQUIRE CREATIVE STORAGE.** Look up and down to use all of your vertical space. Store things under or behind furniture. Use all the available space in closets and cabinets, including the backs of doors. Look into multipurpose furniture like ottomans that function as seating as well as storage, or coffee or end tables with built-in storage spots. These pieces are generally more expensive, but they'll save space—and money—in the long run, because you won't have to pay for additional storage down the road.

- **DON'T GROW YOUR STUFF BEYOND YOUR STORAGE.** Once you have a workable storage system in place, do your best not to expand your stuff beyond the confines of that space. When you start needing to add more storage solutions to a system that you once considered complete, it's probably time to look into paring down your possessions again.

Finding the right balance of stuff and storage is a bit of a tricky game. Don't get stuck in the self-perpetuating cycle of trying to reduce your possessions to less than what you need, but make sure that you have enough room for the stuff you have, and a logical place to put it. With enough thought and effort, you can get to a stuff/storage balance that makes sense and doesn't empty your bank account or force you to tear your home apart trying to accommodate more stuff than you can store. Once everything has a place, you can then move on to keeping everything clean, organized, and comfortable.

CLEANING BASICS

One of the most common reasons people don't clean (coming in a close second after "I don't wanna") is that they don't really know how. There's no small amount of judgment and assumptions associated with people who don't or can't clean. And yes, sometimes it's because someone is lazy or inconsiderate, but those are far from the only reasons someone might not be a great (or good, or even adequate) housekeeper. Sure, cleaning isn't exactly rocket science, but if you never learned how, it can be intimidating as hell, and that's an obstacle to getting started. Not to mention that the longer you go without knowing how to clean, the harder it becomes to obtain those skills. But note that I said "harder," not "impossible." Learning how to clean as an adult is just like learning how to drive a stick shift or communicate in another language: It takes lots of practice, lots of trial and error, and a desire to learn.

There's a plethora of reasons people may not have the skills needed to clean a house, and the environment you're raised in can be one of the biggest contributing factors. Those who grew up in homes where they never learned to clean start out at a disadvantage without those fundamental housekeeping skills. Those who grew up in homes where everything was done for them are also not in a great position. If you come from one of these environments, don't despair! It's not too late.

Fortunately, we live in a time when instructions for just about anything are free and readily available. If you don't know how to do something, it's really easy to find out how. There's an awful lot of really specialized cleaning knowledge to be had out there, but, as in anything, some basics will go a long way toward giving you a solid foundation. Once you have a grasp of some of the fundamental tasks that need to get done, it's fairly straightforward to apply that knowledge to other things you might not have experience with. So if you live in a messy home because you're not quite sure how to keep it from getting or staying that way, there is absolutely hope for you! Don't be ashamed if you don't know this stuff; it's just some skills and knowledge that you haven't acquired yet. There's always more time to learn.

WHAT YOU NEED AND WHAT YOU DON'T

First things first, make sure you're well equipped with the supplies you need to clean. One of the biggest lies sold to you by the cleaning and housekeeping industry is that you need specially designated equipment and products for every task. That's a load of bullshit. Don't fall for it. You don't need expensive or specialized stuff to keep your house clean. You really only need a few very basic things, most of which you might have on hand already. Anyone who recommends a "must-have" product as the only way to accomplish something probably benefits in some way from you buying it. There are some specialized supplies that may make cleaning certain things easier, but they aren't necessary, regardless of what the ads tell you.

At a bare minimum, I could keep a house UfYH-approved clean with just **water, white vinegar, dish soap, some rags or cloths, and a broom.** And laundry detergent, because while you certainly can make your own, that's kind of a huge pain in the ass, and the premade stuff already exists and can be found pretty cheap. Vacuums are great for carpet, but in a pinch, you can absolutely sweep a rug. Just ask my Nana.

Insisting on your need for the "right" tools and products is just another way to put off getting started. It's another excuse to keep yourself from jumping in and doing the best you can with what you have. Make no mistake, you can get a lot, maybe even everything, done using only what you already have or with a few easily and cheaply obtained basics. Don't postpone getting to it any more than you already have by deciding you need to go out, go to the store, stand in the cleaning aisle staring at hundreds of different choices, pick out some stuff, spend a ton of money you don't want to part with, and then go back home, organize it all, and then not ever actually clean anything because you've already done way too much and you're exhausted. That's a pretty tough trap to get out of.

My favorite all-purpose cleaning solution is half hot water, half vinegar, and a glug of dish soap (that's the technical term) mixed up in a spray bottle. Showers, counters, stovetops, toilets— you name it, you can clean it with this, or with one of its components. A combination of time (let the cleaning solution or hot water do the bulk of the work for you by letting it sit for a bit) and a little elbow grease when needed can accomplish just about any cleaning task.

If you're looking for another multipurpose tool that's a little bit more of an investment, consider a steam mop. You can do all of your hard floors with it, and never need anything besides water to use it. Add to that some rags for dusting and wiping down, a broom, a vacuum (if you have carpets), and some laundry detergent, and you're pretty much good to go right away. You don't need a million things, and you don't need to spend a lot of money. With your small but effective arsenal of tools and basics, you're well armed to tackle all the dirt and debris that comes along with living your life.

Oh, I can hear what comes next: "But, bleach!" Most people are absolutely, 100 percent convinced that you cannot clean a house without bleach. I disagree. I think that bleach is generally overused and almost always underdiluted. One of the big problems with bleach is that you shouldn't ever mix it with anything except water. Using bleach and just about anything else together (ammonia-based cleaning products, hydrogen peroxide, vinegar, alcohol, etc.) can create chemical reactions that cause health problems like respiratory issues and skin irritation or burns. **Bleach should only be mixed with water, and it should *always* be mixed with water.** A solution of (at most!) 1:10 bleach:water is the standard recommended dilution for everything up to and including disinfecting. When used correctly and safely, bleach can be quite useful, but it's not necessary, even for disinfecting. In the United States, the Environmental Protection Agency (EPA) tests and labels products as "sanitizing" or "disinfecting," so read your labels if you're looking to disinfect without using bleach.

And what about convenience items like sanitizing wipes and

single-use dusters and the like? No one is going to dispute that these things can be terrible for the environment, and they can get pretty expensive, too. But if wipes are going to mean the difference between cleaning your house or not, wipe away and figure out how to offset the environmental impact in another way. There's already a lot of guilt wrapped up in cleaning; don't let arguments against convenience items deter you from getting stuff done. Convenience cleaning products exist for a reason: They're convenient. They save time and effort. They don't make you a bad person. Life is full of balances and compromises, so just figure out how to balance convenience with environmental and financial responsibility.

There are plenty of DIY solutions for making your own cleaning wipes and such, but it's totally OK if you don't have the energy, time, or inclination to do so. We don't all live in an ideal world of frugality and environmentalism, armed with the ability and desire to create every consumer item from scratch. So use whatever tools you have at your disposal to get the job done, and let go of the guilt. There are always going to be people who disagree with this, who think that disposable products are always bad and have no place; if you're one of those people, don't use them. Simple. If you're someone who needs to use these products, especially when you're just getting started, do what you need to do and try not to get wrapped up in guilt about it.

Try, too, not to get caught up in the "natural" trap. The problem with terms like "natural" and "toxic" and "chemical" is that these days, they're all essentially meaningless. Don't fool yourself: Everything is a chemical, even water. "Chemical" doesn't mean bad, and "natural" doesn't mean good. Lots of things are "natural" that you wouldn't want to be in extended contact with, like poison ivy and hornets and manure, and lots of "natural" things are also "toxic," like botulism and deadly mushrooms. Be a discerning consumer when it comes to your products, and also be wary of jargon and buzzwords. Don't get drawn in by something just because it's labeled "natural" or pushed away because someone on the Internet said that something is a "toxic chemical." These terms are overused and misused to the point of being useless. They're just another way to manipulate you into consuming what someone wants to sell you. Learn to recognize these buzzwords for what they are: ultimately nonsensical and an attempt to elicit an emotional and financial reaction without much examination on the part of the consumer.

WHERE TO BEGIN

Most people say their biggest problem with cleaning is that they don't know where to start. And when you're staring down a whole-house mess with no end in sight, it's definitely a logical concern. It's difficult to prioritize where to start or what's most important. If you're stuck at the beginning, **a good rule of thumb is to start with stuff that smells bad or has the potential to smell bad.** So garbage, dishes, and laundry, then. If you're lucky enough to have a washer and dryer in your home, start a load of laundry first thing. If doing laundry requires hauling everything to the Laundromat, gather all your dirty clothes and your laundry supplies together and make an appointment with yourself for a few hours to go deal with it—and then follow through! Continue by collecting all of the obvious trash and recycling that you can, and remove it from your house entirely. Then gather up dishes and put them in the sink to soak; this will make washing them later a whole lot easier. Keep in mind that laundry and dishes have three steps: *wash, dry, and put it away, goddammit!* Once those three things have been taken care of, you're moving firmly from "dirty" to "messy," and that's a big deal.

If there's something in your home that causes you a disproportionate amount of stress (and yes, sometimes this is going to be "everything," but see if one specific thing jumps out at you), this might be where you need to start, regardless of whether or not it's the worst or stinkiest or messiest. Sometimes, mentally, you just need to get the thing that's bothering you the most out of the way before you can even start to think about moving on to something else. I'm a big proponent of starting with the thing you're dreading the most. Not only do you get it done and over with right away before it has the chance to take over any more of your time and attention, but you give yourself the opportunity to feel like such a rock star when you've vanquished your housekeeping white whale. Once you've done what previously seemed impossible, everything else seems a little bit more attainable and a little less scary. Having a dreaded task hanging over your head can make everything else seem much more difficult than it actually is, so go ahead and just get it done first. Once the big, scary thing is done, the mental block that's preventing you from moving on to the next thing may very well disappear.

WHAT TO DO AND WHEN

Once you have the tools and supplies you need to get going, and you know where to start, now what? How, exactly, do you clean? It's one of those things that seems like it should be incredibly obvious to everyone everywhere, but if you never learned how to clean, it's like trying to read a book that everyone around you loves but is written in a language that you've never seen before.

Fortunately, it's pretty straightforward, and here are a few tips that will help you begin to tackle any mess:

- **Work from top to bottom. Floors should be the last thing you clean.**

- **Start with your largest flat surface. Clear it off and then move on to the next flat surface.**

- **Clean dry before you clean wet. For example, dust before wiping with a damp cloth, and sweep before mopping.**

The great thing about cleaning is that even if you do it "wrong," it's rarely, if ever, a catastrophe. Even if you have absolutely no idea how to clean, as long as whatever you're cleaning ends up less dirty than when you started, you win! Sure, it is *technically* possible to really get it wrong, but, in general, as long as you stay away from scrubbing or scouring something to the point of damage, using a too-harsh cleaning solution, smashing things apart, or lighting things on fire, you're probably OK. It might not be ideal, maybe it could be cleaner, but it's definitely not the end of the world if it ain't perfect. So allow yourself to make some mistakes while you're learning. The trial-and-error process is great because as you're learning, things are getting clean! Win/win!

Once you learn how to clean stuff, the next thing to tackle is how often to clean different things. An easy cheat to remember is that things that are unusable after one use or so need to be cleaned *as they're used*. So that means dishes, some clothes, and litter boxes (cats tend to have stricter standards for "clean" than most humans). What you use every day should be cleaned at least weekly. The shower, the toilet, and the sheets fall into that category. For just about everything else, monthly or as needed is usually fine. Remember that the intervals that work for you and your life may not match up with what other lists and schedules are telling you. When you're first getting started, err on the side of more often, and then scale back and adjust as needed. For example, if you wear a uniform to work, laundry once a week may not cut it. You might need to wash clothes every two days. Don't get too wrapped up in how often someone else, even me, tells you to clean things. Come up with a plan that works for you, and then stick with it.

A critical part of figuring out when to do things is realizing that cleaning is a continuous cycle. You're going to clean everything, and it's going to look great and beautiful, but then you're going to continue living your life, and it's going to get messed up again. This doesn't mean you're a failure. It's just what happens. There is no one alive who is such a great housekeeper that they only have to clean things once ever. In fact, the measure of success of someone's housekeeping ability is probably that they manage to do things at exactly the right intervals. Because, say it with me, *nothing stays clean forever.* You use your home, so it gets messy and dirty and needs to be cleaned again. It can be incredibly discouraging to see all of your hard work come undone just from regular life happening, but don't get too down on yourself about it. There's no way to avoid it, and it happens to all of us. The best you can do is to clean often enough that the mess doesn't get too terrible before it's time to reset to clean again.

SMALL SPACES

S o, you might be sitting in your dorm room, studio apartment, or bedroom in someone else's house, having read this far, and thinking, "This advice is fine, I guess, but I don't have a whole freaking house!" Fair enough. Trying to maintain an entire existence's worth of stuff in a tiny little space brings its own set of annoying problems. When you're dealing with a smaller space like a dorm room or a single bedroom, every single bit of organization becomes critically important. When you have less space overall to deal with, a little bit of a mess looks pretty huge. You have to be smarter and more creative about storage. You need to pare down your belongings and keep only what's useful and loved. Easy, right? Just kidding! It sucks! It can be pretty difficult to maintain a clean and organized environment in a space better suited for tiny garden gnomes than actual human beings, but it can be done.

ONLY KEEP WHAT YOU NEED

Is there anything good about a small living space? Of course there is. It takes a lot less effort to keep it clean. Everything takes just a fraction of the time. Maintenance is considerably less involved, even though it's more frequent. You don't have to dedicate huge amounts of time to keep small spaces clean. You don't have to start over again in a whole bunch of different rooms. You just need to think on a smaller scale and reexamine your habits and schedules in order to keep on top of a smaller space.

To start with, when you're dealing with such limited space, you won't need half the shit you have. The best, most effective way to keep things clean and organized in a small space is to have less stuff. By paring down your possessions, you make your cleaning and maintenance much easier. But this isn't the time to get overwhelmed with some minimalist ideal. Remember that your goal isn't to have *no* possessions, but to really think critically about what you need and what you'll use. Unnecessary items will just add to the chaos, give you more to have to pick up and store on a regular basis, and reduce the usable space in your room, so try to bring into the space only things that are needed and useful. (Be honest with yourself about this!) When you start out with only necessary and useful items, you reduce the number of things you need to store, hide, maintain, or otherwise deal with. If you're already in the space and have more things than you reasonably have space for, your first step is going to involve figuring out what, of all those things, it's necessary for you to hang on to.

USE YOUR STORAGE SPACE WISELY

In a small space, in addition to reducing the amount of stuff you have, it's absolutely critical to maximize your storage. Even more importantly, you should be matching your storage to your stuff. When your space is clean, every item should have a place—preferably one that's stashed away somewhere and not out on display. To accomplish this, you should ideally be using every space you can find: under things, behind things, and even above things. Use vertical space wherever possible, and never under-estimate how much shit you can fit under a bed, especially if you can manage to elevate the bed a little bit. Tension rods, hooks, and flat storage are infinitely useful in small spaces. Small spaces require creativity, so look at every possible square inch for how it can be useful to you.

If you have a closet, make sure you're using it to its full advantage. Most people just use a small part of the available space in their closets: the hanging bar, the floor, maybe a shelf above the hanging bar. But there's so much more space you can be uti-lizing. If you have a shelf above the hanging bar, don't just put some stuff on it and call it a day. Create another level or two of storage with modular shelves, baskets, dividers, or boxes. Same thing with the closet floor. At the very least, you can stack shoe boxes on the floor, and with just a little more effort, you can create more complex storage with shelving and storage boxes. Using the closet floor for shoe storage is really common, but shoes take up a lot of available "floorage" and waste just as much. If you have a lot of shoes to store, it's worth it to come up with a space-maximizing storage system that doesn't just occupy all of your floor space.

There's even more closet storage space that most people don't think to use. The interior walls and the ceiling can hold a bunch of items with the help of hooks or bars. The inside of a closet door can be utilized when you employ hanging storage. Even the hanging bar can do double or triple duty with hanging storage for shoes, accessories, or even folded clothes, or bars that create a second level for hanging clothes. There are plenty of commercial closet organization solutions available, but you don't need to spend a ton of money on this stuff. Most can be improvised at home with stuff you already have, or found at discount stores for much less. Since it's all going to be behind a closed door, you don't need to worry so much about everything matching perfectly. Closets are great because you can fit so much shit in them, and then you can just close the door and hide everything.

Speaking of which, try to hide as much as you can. Remember that open storage can look very messy, especially when you're dealing with a smaller space. Shelves and such are great for maximizing how much stuff you can fit into a smaller space, but when that storage is open and on display, it doesn't necessarily make things look neater and more streamlined. Enclosed storage will make everything look a little bit neater simply because it's out of the way. Matching storage is great but expensive, so try to focus on getting everything stashed so that it's hidden but still accessible when you need it. As always, set up your storage in a logical way: Things you use the most need to be the most accessible, while less frequently used items can be tucked away in places that are harder to get to. Storage spots that are difficult to reach should be reserved for the stuff you won't need to access often. Use your drawers and closets to the best advantage that you can, but don't just cram them full of stuff, because the first time you need to get something out, you're going to end up with stuff strewn everywhere, and once it's out of its hiding spot, the likelihood of it getting back in there is pretty slim.

If you have limited (or no) closet space, things become a little bit trickier, but by no means impossible. Without closet space, your storage situation may have to rely on shelves, freestanding furniture, and other open-storage means. In this situation, too, it's good to try to hide things; just keep in mind that it might require additional storage pieces like boxes and baskets. Without closet space, it may be worth investing in a covered or enclosed clothing rack to provide much-needed hanging space (and hide it, at least a little). Of course, that involves spending money that you may not have, so if that's not an option, it can totally be worked around. Just reexamine your drawer and cabinet space in freestanding pieces like dressers, as well as maximizing space under, above, and behind other things.

FIND SOME HIDDEN STORAGE

- **Walk around your room and identify one spot that's currently being wasted that could be used for storage. This can be under or behind existing furniture, inside a closet, or on top of something else. Once you've identified a space, go ahead and move some stuff there and see how it works.**

EVERYTHING IN ITS PLACE

As far as habits go, there's nothing more important than "don't put it down, put it away." This is so crucial in small spaces. When you return every item to its predetermined home, you drastically cut down on visible clutter and keep everything looking streamlined and clean. Of course, this assumes that everything has a predetermined home, so if you don't have that planned out and squared away, make it your first priority. When you know where everything is going back to, you save yourself a lot of mental and physical energy by not having to work out a plan every single time you put something away. "A place for everything and everything in its place" may be one of Aunt Edna's annoying old adages that makes you roll your eyes, but when you're dealing with limited space and a desire to keep it clean, it's actually pretty relevant.

You're also going to need to do maintenance way more frequently. One or two things out of place can create a huge amount of visual chaos in a small space, so your maintenance habits are going to be vital. Resetting things back to clean daily will be incredibly helpful, as will keeping to a maintenance routine more frequently than perhaps you'd like. Yes, having to pick up or clean once or twice a day, every day, may suck a little bit, but letting things go for a few days becomes much less of an option in a small space. Getting used to doing a small amount of cleaning more frequently will greatly cut down on how often you'll need to do a huge, total-room clean. Not to mention that the amount of time and effort involved is really quite minimal. We're talking just a few minutes every day, something that can be accomplished during a commercial break or while dancing to one guilty-pleasure pop song.

Also keep in mind that in a small space, garbage, laundry, and dishes need to be dealt with ASAP. There's not only the clutter aspect to deal with, but those things also have the potential to get stinky and gross, fast. By keeping on top of them, you can keep the funk away and discourage little critter friends from moving in and making themselves at home. (Once ants, cockroaches, fruit flies, or mice move in, getting rid of them is time-consuming and soul-crushing. Better to just prevent the problem entirely.) It can be a tough habit to build, but dealing with your dishes and trash immediately and your dirty laundry regularly and frequently is probably the biggest thing you can do to keep things from getting out-of-control messy.

And when it comes to laundry, don't forget about the floordrobe. Oh, God, the floordrobe. This is absolutely one of the biggest ways that small spaces go to shit very quickly. In a small space, every piece of clothing flung to the floor increases the chaos by a huge percentage. One of the best ways to keep your room looking clean, even if it really isn't all that clean, is to keep the floor clear. Put dirty clothes in the hamper, and put clean clothes away. Don't even begin to consider your floor as free-standing storage for your clothing. It's not. It's a place for you to walk and to put your furniture on. It's not a dresser, it's not a garbage can, and if you aren't careful, it can breed mess like you wouldn't believe. One pair of socks leads to a whole outfit leads to every article of clothing you own strewn about the place. Put your clothes away. Defeat the floordrobe.

MINI-CHALLENGE

- **Take ten minutes and reset as much as you can back to clean. Put items away, throw trash out, and hang up or put away your clothes until the timer goes off.**

DORM-ROOM DRAMA

If you're in a dorm room and sharing with another person, all of these problems have the potential to end up twice as bad. Keep in mind that you will be tripping over each other's shit all the time, so it's in your best interest to come up with a plan to deal with it before you inevitably start hating each other. Small spaces plus people who barely know each other equals a recipe for disaster. The best way to avoid (or at least mitigate) most roommate problems is to anticipate them and make a plan for what happens when something arises. One of the most common things that causes strife between roommates is differing standards and effort regarding cleanliness. Ignoring this or pretending you're somehow going to be the one exception to roommate drama is a surefire way to set yourself up for conflict and aggravation.

The close quarters of a dorm room can compound all roommate issues, mainly because you're already tripping over each other on a near-constant basis. When there's conflict between two people living in a tiny room, everything seems so much worse because there's nowhere you can retreat to, no door you can close between you and the problem. It's even more important when you live in a dorm, then, to start out with a solid plan so that two (or more) people plus no real personal space doesn't have to equal resentment and anger.

It may seem juvenile and unnecessary, but a chore list can be just the tool you need to keep your dorm-room situation from devolving into a screaming hellscape of animosity and filth. It's nonjudgmental, unemotional, and straightforward. Once you figure out who's going to do what and when, there's no need for arguments or passive-aggressive behavior (at least when it comes to the state of your room). Nevertheless, problems will arise, and a written agreement can help you deal with them. Don't be naïve and think that you'll be able to cruise through a roommate situation without anyone getting resentful or angry. It always happens. Best to walk into the situation with open eyes and fully prepared to handle the inevitable.

Before dividing up the chores, sit down and have a conversation. Figure out if there are any tasks one of you doesn't mind doing at all, and which ones you loathe with every fiber of your being. Then determine the general magnitude of each task. An equitable division of chores isn't necessarily going to result from having the same *number* of tasks; it's the time investment that matters. "Big" chores and "small" chores, depending on how much time and effort they require, should be divided up so that neither of you feels like you're shouldering the majority of the work.

SMALL SPACES, BIG PROBLEMS!

If you're in the super-fun situation of living in a small space within someone else's larger space, like a room at your parents' home or a rented room within a shared home, you have the added complication of having some items in common spaces that are not entirely under your control. All of the same principles still apply—maximize your storage, pick up a little every day—plus all of the stuff you need to do in common spaces. Once again, dishes and trash are really important. Make sure you're keeping on top of those, not just in your own space but in common spaces as well. Doing your part to reset and deal with your effect on common spaces is a necessary part of these kinds of living situations.

That said, you may find that the common spaces are messier than you'd like, or that your possessions aren't being respected. Like all shared-living problems, this one isn't ever going to get better until you talk about it. Have a conversation with the preset goals of defining everyone's roles and responsibilities in creating a clean and harmonious living situation. Keep in mind that if you don't like people messing with your stuff, that goes both ways. If, during your discussion, a workable plan for handling the common spaces arises, great! But it might not.

If the person or people whom the space ultimately belongs to don't want to change their messy ways, the best you can do is advocate for yourself and your place in the home, deal with your own stuff and your own mess, and decide if the living situation is something you can deal with. You may also want to focus your housekeeping efforts primarily on whatever small space you can call your own. Keeping your own room/space cleaned up to your own standards may be the most control you have over the situation, so if that's the only place you can focus your attention, do that. Make your small part of the larger space a comfortable and happy space for yourself, and try to let go of being stressed out by what other people do with their stuff. Of course, you have the right to a comfortable place to live, so if the expectations and standards are drastically different between you and whoever you share space with, it might not be a livable situation for you.

PARENTAL UNITS

Unlike in most other shared-space arrangements like being roommates or living with a significant other, there's a considerable power imbalance when adult children live with their parents. "My house, my rules" is easily the most common refrain when children, regardless of age, live in their parents' home, but that can be a damaging mindset fraught with problems that extend beyond sharing a home and into the familial relationship. While, yes, it's a logical viewpoint, it also ignores the fact that we all have the right to enjoy where we live with a modicum of autonomy.

There are any number of reasons adult children may live with their parents: cultural norms, financial limitations, etc. When children have moved away and then move back, it can be difficult to reframe the parent/child relationship in a way that respects both the parents' authority over the home and the child's autonomy as an adult. As in every other shared living situation, the best way to come to an arrangement that works for everyone involved is to talk about it. Have a frank and honest conversation about expectations and responsibilities. With frequent and productive communication, this living arrangement doesn't have to be full of emotional minefields.

One of the more difficult things to deal with when living as an adult in your parents' home can be accepting that you only have control over a very small part of where you live. The house as a whole is not yours, so it may be tough to exert any kind of power over the living conditions in general. What you can do, though, is make your room into a haven that you truly enjoy. With good storage, a strong organizational system, and by staying on top of keeping it clean and tidy, you can turn your one room into a mini-home that you enjoy spending time in, without having to stress out about all of the other rooms that are still firmly under your parents' jurisdiction.

LIVING IN SMALL spaces doesn't have to mean a cluttered, chaotic environment. With a small amount of effort and a solid plan for getting and staying organized, a small space can be just as comfortable, clean, and inviting as a whole house. And while having to pick up and clean more often can be kind of annoying, it also almost completely eradicates the need for stressed-out marathon cleaning. So whether you're in a dorm, a tiny studio apartment, or just one room in someone else's house, you can still very easily make that space your own and keep it from devolving into a disaster zone. You just have to get started.

3

TROUBLESHOOTING: DEALING WITH OTHER PEOPLE IN YOUR FUCKED-UP SPACE

Roommates, Spouses, and Significant Others

Asking for Help or Helping Someone Else

ROOMMATES, SPOUSES, AND SIGNIFICANT OTHERS

Congratulations! You've decided to turn your messy home into a place that you love to spend time in. You have the tools you need to get started with a sustainable cleaning plan, you're motivated, you're energized, you're excited. For the first time, you feel like there might be hope for you and your home after all. There's just one little problem: You live with other people. Whether those people are connected to you by blood, by choice, or by the fact that rent is really freaking expensive, adding other human beings into the equation will always complicate things. And these complications are rarely for the better.

Let's just get the cold, hard truth out of the way right off the bat: Living with other people is pretty much the worst. Regardless of your relationship, you and the people you live with probably fight the most about two things: money and housekeeping. That's true for spouses, roommates, parents and children, whatever. But the housekeeping part of it doesn't have to be that bad. If you can understand why you fight about housekeeping, and make an effort to either prevent or resolve these conflicts, you just might be able to survive a shared living space. Who knows? You might even be able to enjoy it. Maybe.

The difficult, shitty reality of living with other people is that it sucks because you're sharing space with people whose standards and habits often do not align with your own. When two or more people are sharing a living area, one person almost always has a much stricter standard for "clean," and they're almost always angry about it. Angry because the person or people they live with aren't maintaining the same standard; angry because someone invariably feels like they're doing all of the work; angry because they don't see the point in putting all of this work in around the house if no one's going to help them, dammit! There's always a perceived inequity in effort toward housework: One person feels like another isn't doing their part, or one person feels like another has unreasonable and unrealistic expectations of them, and both of these situations breed resentment and rage. But they don't have to.

Whether you live with roommates, a spouse, children, your parents, or in any other configuration of shared housing, your relationships with the people you live with can affect how you progress with getting your mess under control. Your main goals in living with other people should be sticking to your own habits and routines, using open and frequent communication to ask for help or buy-in or just understanding, and accepting the limits that exist when you involve other people. If you can keep your frustration, anger, or resentment to a minimum, you'll be much more successful and much happier in your home overall. And the best way to avoid all of those negative emotions is to just get everything out in the open before it has a chance to fester and get worse.

While navigating the obstacle course that is living with other people, it's good to remember a few key points:

YOU CAN'T CHANGE ANYONE'S HABITS BUT YOUR OWN

You can beg for help, plead for buy-in, make threats, stomp around, throw things, or just generally despair of your situation, but the sad fact is that you can't make someone care about the mess the same way that you care about the mess. If you live with loved ones, hopefully you can make them care about how the mess affects *you,* since they presumably already care about your feelings, but as far as changing habits goes, you're better off focusing your energies inward. It's important to realize that this is a personal journey, and getting upset or resentful about what other people are or aren't doing can be a major setback in your own progress. You'll start focusing more on what everyone else is or isn't doing than on making changes within yourself, and that's a surefire path to disappointment.

It can be difficult to let go of this mindset, but your time is better spent working on your own habits; eventually, the people you live with just might come around. Until then, though, do this for you. Do it because you want somewhere nice to live, and because you deserve the satisfaction of being the one to make it that way.

YOU'RE THE ONE WHO'S INVESTED IN THIS RIGHT NOW

You're ready to go. You've done your reading, you've armed your-self with the necessary supplies and plans, and you're so excited to get going. Unfortunately, this doesn't mean that the people you live with are at the same point. If they are, that's great, and it makes everything easier for everyone. But chances are, you're revved up and they aren't. They might be skeptical, or annoyed, or pessimistic. Maybe they just don't even give a shit at all. That's fine. That's on them. What you need to focus on is you and your behavior and habits. If you're successful, chances are good that they'll come around. In the meantime, don't let the fact that you seem to be in this alone deter you. Just because the people you live with don't share your enthusiasm doesn't mean you can't succeed. You just might have to be your own cheerleader for a while.

And just because the other people in your home aren't on your level as far as the process goes doesn't make them the enemy. It's easy to frame a situation like this as "me vs. them," but that's not really a helpful mindset. Understand that their not being as psyched up as you are about cleaning the house doesn't mean they want you to fail. It just means that you have different levels of investment, with yours being pretty high and theirs ranging anywhere from "meh" to nonexistent. Don't take it personally. It's not a reflection on how they feel about you; it's a reflection on how they feel about housework.

IT'S NOT SABOTAGE; EITHER THEY DON'T NOTICE OR THEY DON'T CARE

This one can sting a little, I know. But there are very few instances in which someone you live with is actively trying to sabotage your efforts. If that's truly the case, then it's probably time to start reexamining your living situation, because that's some toxic bullshit right there. In the vast majority of circumstances, however, it's far more likely that the people who share your home either don't realize what it is you're doing, or they notice it but it's not a particularly high priority for them.

Again, this isn't personal. It's not about you. It's about them. And the best you can do is acknowledge that they're not *intentionally* making things worse for you, even if things getting worse is the ultimate result. Don't assume sabotage when obliviousness is the more likely answer. Human beings are inclined to attribute things to malice that are best explained by apathy, and when we falsely identify other people's motivations, we create a situation in our minds that not only doesn't exist but colors all of our future interactions. Avoid this. Talk about it. If they don't notice, tell them. If they don't care, make it plain that you do.

SERIOUSLY, TALK ABOUT IT

The vast majority of problems with roommates (and with relationships of all kinds, to be honest) can usually be solved with conversation. Sitting down and talking, rather than letting things build up and risking miscommunication, will go a long way toward avoiding or resolving conflict of all kinds. It's no different when you're dealing with housework.

The best time to have a conversation about housework

expectations and potential problems is *before* you enter into a living situation with other people. The second-best time is right now. You're never going to make any progress whatsoever with the people you share space with if you don't sit down and talk to them. And I mean a real, verbal conversation. None of this leaving notes nonsense. You know that's passive-aggressive. Any potential progress will be dashed from the outset if you leave a note instead of having a talk.

If you're lucky enough to be able to have the discussion before entering into a shared living situation, use the time to discuss everyone's expectations. Come up with a schedule or a list or a chart, whichever works best for you. Most important, come up with a plan for what to do when things inevitably go off the rails. That way, when it's three days after the trash was supposed to have been taken out and it's still sitting there stinking up the kitchen, you have a mutually agreed-upon course of action to address it.

If you're already living with people and things need to change, sit down and talk it out as soon as possible. This discussion can be far more difficult, because it carries the weight of past experience with it, so it's critically important to try to keep accusations and resentment out of it. Think of it as a reset; you're looking to change things, starting now. You can't change what's happened in the past, no matter how much you might want to. Follow the steps you'd take for an initial discussion: Figure out who's going to do what and when. Decide, together, what to do when things get off track. Be honest about expectations and workload. And again, if you live with family—either chosen or by blood—rather than roommates, use the fact that you care about and value each other to help move your discussion along. If someone cares about you but doesn't care about the mess, try explaining how the mess affects you, and how they can help, not necessarily because *they* want the mess gone, but because they care about your happiness and sanity.

This conversation is rarely easy, and maybe it won't go the way that you're hoping. The important thing is to have it. Lay out your plans and your hopes, and figure out how much buy-in you're going to get from the people you live with. Knowing this ahead of time can help you temper your expectations and come up with a clear game plan for dealing with all of the things that might arise as you try to get your mess under control. If your conversation ends in you figuring out you're on your own in this, well, at least you have an informed baseline to work with, and you can make decisions about what you do and don't do from there. If you need some pointers for getting a conversation started, flip to "Dividing up the work: Talking points for difficult conversations" in the Resources section.

DON'T BE A DOORMAT

If the people you live with aren't being cooperative, no one's saying you need to be the maid. No one's saying you need to constantly be cleaning up after the people you live with. You can work around other people and their stuff without having to become responsible for it. When you have a solid, clear plan, it's very easy to know how you need to interact with other people's stuff. If your conversation is thorough enough, you'll know exactly how to respond when your roommate leaves dishes in the sink for two weeks, or what to do with a couch piled with laundry that isn't yours. Clear communication will help you avoid feeling like you're doing all the work or you're stuck being responsible for everyone else's stuff.

Part of being the one to get the mess under control when other people are involved is that you have to be the one to initiate the crappy conversations. Rather than taking all of your roommate's dirty dishes and dumping them on their bed (I understand the inclination, really, I do, but I mean, come on), you need to say, "I need to wash my dishes, but yours are taking up all of the space in the sink. When can I expect the sink to be available for me?" If, at that point, your roommate tells you they don't care if you put the dishes on their bed, well, then go ahead and do that. Don't take responsibility for the dishes, but make it perfectly clear that they need to be dealt with.

Does it suck to have to hold adults accountable for their own belongings? Absolutely. Is it frustrating to be the one who always has to take charge and initiate these conversations? No doubt. But part of living and interacting with other people is taking responsibility for your own priorities by making your needs clear. Make no mistake: There are shitty roommates out there. Lots of them. There are people who simply won't do their part no matter how many reasonable conversations you have. But unfortunately, whether it's for the rest of the lease or until you can afford to move out, you have to live there. Don't sacrifice your sanity. Take whatever steps you need to in order to ensure a comfortable living space for yourself in the meantime. And who knows? To someone else, maybe you're the shitty roommate. It's all about perception, and it's good to realize that people are complex in their interactions with each other and often end up showing parts of their personalities they aren't proud of, like spite and anger and pettiness, as a reaction to what their living environment is like.

Feeling like a doormat when you're living with kids

Those of you who have children may find yourself feeling like a doormat more often than not. "I'm not the parent," you think, "I'm the maid!" Well, now is the time to start changing that dynamic. Keep in mind that unless you won some kind of parenting jackpot, your kids are probably going to: A) absolutely hate cleaning; B) complain and whine about it and throw tantrums and tell you they hate you for making them put their stuff away; and C) be pretty terrible at cleaning, because they're kids and they're still learning both how to clean and how to not be intentionally awful at stuff they really don't want to do.

Consistency, patience, positivity, and clear expectations are all important when you're trying to bring kids of all ages in line with your "Holy crap, I need you people to help me out here" plan. Resist the urge to throw up your hands and just do it yourself when things aren't going as you'd like, because then you're just training your kids in the dark art of learned helplessness. If you start young enough, this process will be easier. Not 100 percent easy, because what about parenting is easy? But if you're not at the point where you need to untrain bad habits or remove the expectation that House Adult does all the cleaning while the kids play Mario Kart, said kids will learn that they might not like your expectations, but they do still have to do what you ask, and video games are not going to happen until all the toys are back in their homes.

Being positive about housework can go a long way toward teaching your kids how to clean. If you're perpetually annoyed and frustrated by housework and that's what the kids are seeing, they're gonna learn real quick that housework is a thing to be feared and hated, not unlike a punishment. By not treating cleaning and housework like, well, a chore, you'll make it a little easier to get them into the habit of meeting your expectations and keeping a clean house to boot. Praise and rewards, even small ones, go a long way toward reinforcing good behavior. Even if the job is imperfectly done, it's so important to reward effort rather than criticizing results. With time and practice, they'll eventually get better at housework, and being supported and congratulated even after less-than-desired results will help encourage them to keep trying. And by modeling positivity when doing housework yourself, instead of letting your aggravation and annoyance show, you'll teach your kids that it's just a normal part of life.

If you have or live with children and you're trying to teach them to pick up after themselves, keep in mind that how you interact with them regarding housework will likely shape the way they approach cleaning for the rest of their lives. In the beginning, the routine and the effort are far more important than the end result. The more critical you are, the more likely they are to develop negative associations with cleaning that could affect them even years later. Encourage effort above all. Sure, you can direct them toward the most effective way of doing something, but if you recognize and celebrate their efforts rather than criticizing their results, then housekeeping will become just another thing to do, rather than a dreaded chore, a punishment, or an activity to rebel against.

PASSIVE-AGGRESSIVE BEHAVIOR
NEVER WORKS

Put the Post-it notes down and step away. Stop muttering under your breath. Take it easy on slamming the cabinet doors. These are all really common reactions to frustration at other people not pulling their weight, but unfortunately, without exception, they're all completely ineffective. Passive-aggressive acts come across as petty, they undermine your position as far as asking for help, they cause the object of your behavior to be defensive, and they make you seem childish and irrational. But, for some reason, we keep thinking that leaving nasty notes and mumbling through our frustrations is the most effective way to get through to people who aren't doing what we want them to. Nope, it's avoidance dressed up in fancy attire. Slamming things and stomping around because you aren't pleased with how things are going comes across as childish for a reason: because you're basically throwing a low-grade temper tantrum. It may feel good in the short term to get the frustration out, but it will almost never result in any actual change in your situation.

Listen, passive-aggressive behavior will almost always backfire on you. Either the person you're mad at won't even realize what you're doing, or they'll swing all the way back around to *actively* not helping because they're so annoyed. Use your energy more wisely and have an actual adult conversation. Start a dialogue, explain what's upsetting you, ask for specific things that will help you, and really listen to what the other person has to say. You may find out that your expectations are out of line with reality, or that, shockingly, other people have no idea what's going on in your head unless you sit down and tell them. Many people go straight to passive-aggressive behavior without trying any other, more effective methods first, simply because they don't realize that not everyone has the same standards and expectations that they do.

Passive-aggressive behavior comes in other flavors, too. A lot of people tend to just stop cleaning when they get fed up with the people who live with them, figuring, "I'll show them how bad it can get when I don't do everything!" This is counterproductive on a whole bunch of levels. First of all, as we've already addressed, it's possible that they won't notice or won't care. And if they do notice, your actions are just going to come across as spiteful and petty. Not to mention, when you do this, you also have to live in the mess while you're busy making your point. You're punishing yourself just as much as you imagine you're punishing the people you live with. More, even, because the mess bothers you in a way it obviously doesn't bother them. Lots of people do the spite strike. Don't do the spite strike. Have a conversation instead.

LET GO OF "THE RIGHT WAY"

"The right way" here means "the way I would do it, and therefore the only possible way anyone should do it." If you're looking for help around the house, you might have to unclench a little bit and realize that there's more than one way of loading a dishwasher, or cleaning a toilet, or doing laundry. When someone makes an effort to help only to be told that they're doing it wrong, do you think that inspires them to want to pitch in more? No, it absolutely does not. It tells them that no matter what they do, it won't be good enough, so why bother? Imposing your own standards on someone else is hardly an effective way to make them want to do their part.

If you're holding someone to your exact standards of "clean," you may need to step back a little bit and ask, "Is it clean enough, even if it's not the way I think it should be done?" People who complain about lack of help are often sabotaging themselves by doing everything possible to make sure that the people they want to help are so discouraged and dejected that they never try again. Either relax a little about things being done "the right way," or give up the right to complain that you aren't getting any help.

If you're the person who's on the receiving end of criticism, first figure out if you're intentionally half-assing the task because you don't feel like doing it, or if you're actually doing the best you can. If you're not putting in a legitimate effort, ask yourself why, and whether it would be just as easy (and cause less grief) to do it right. If you are doing your best but still falling short of someone else's expectations, talk to that person. You might ask them to cut you a little slack since you're legitimately putting in the effort. Tell them that their criticism makes it difficult to want to help out more, since you feel like what you're doing isn't good enough. See if you can come to some sort of accord and help them see that you are, in fact, trying.

IF YOU'RE THE "OTHER" ONE . . .

So, the person you live with is trying to clean up your home, and now they're trying to get you to help, too. What the hell? How dare they, right? Come on, let's be fair here. No one is under the impression that anyone actually wants to clean. But sometimes it needs to happen, and if you're contributing to making the mess, it's not unreasonable to expect you to help clean it up.

And, yes, maybe you feel like for whatever reason it shouldn't be your job. Maybe you really, truly don't care if the place is messy. You don't mind dirty laundry, a dearth of clean dishes doesn't bug you at all, and you don't care if other people see the place as the grungy landscape it is (or you have no interest in inviting people over, ever). Having a clean house is honestly the least important thing to you, so why should you have to participate in cleaning up? Well, guess what? You participated in making the mess, and it's obviously at least kind of important to the person or people you live with. And depending on your relationship with said person or people, that can give you some reasonably compelling reasons to help out.

If it's your roommate trying to get you to clean up, keep in mind that you're both paying to live there, and your roommate isn't paying for the privilege of dealing with your mess. As part of the basic social contract of living with someone, you owe it to them to, at the very least, keep your own mess confined to your personal space. That means doing your own dishes, making sure your mess doesn't infringe on shared spaces, and not using their stuff and then leaving it for them to deal with. Let me repeat that: *Do not use your roommate's stuff and then leave it for them to deal with.* This means *not* using their dishes and leaving them dirty, *not* eating their food and leaving them to replace it, and *not* wearing their clothes and leaving them unwashed (weird, but . . . it happens). Even if you have express permission to use their dishes, eat their food, or wear their clothes, basic courtesy dictates that you return things to people in the condition you received them, or replace things that you used up.

When you live with someone, even if you don't particularly like them, there's a ground-floor expectation for your behavior: the bare minimum of consideration you'd show anyone else in their own home (even when that home is your home, too). If you're being asked to do things that you legitimately feel are unreasonable, rather than going on some kind of strike, explain that you'll be happy to wash dishes, but once a day is far more realistic than three times a day. Or that cleaning the bathroom is doable, but on the weekend works much better for you than in the middle of a workweek.

Relationships require communication and compromise from all participants. It's a dick move to share a living space with someone and think that you have zero responsibility toward keeping that space clean, but if you have real reasons why you need to adapt or adjust what you're being asked to do, sit down and have a conversation about it. Your living environment will be far more bearable—maybe even pleasant!—if you and your roommate can hash things out in a way that doesn't leave either of you feeling like the other is being unreasonable.

If the person you live with is your spouse or significant other, you have to consider that you have a relationship that's far more important than being roommates. Knowing that, however, doesn't change the fact that people in romantic relationships who cohabitate always fight about housekeeping. Always. Cleaning and money are, by far, the most common topics of arguments between romantic partners, and what often ends up destroying these relationships isn't relationship issues but roommate ones. The added nuances of a romantic relationship usually end up making roommate stuff *more* complicated rather than less, because there are so many levels of interpersonal conflicts and emotions that inform every little household issue. So when you're fighting about the dishes, you're not just fighting about the dishes. You're fighting about what the dishes *represent*.

While you may not care about the mess, if your partner is asking (or begging) for help, *your partner* cares about the mess. And you need to decide whether or not you care about your partner and their feelings more than you *don't* care about the mess. If not contributing to household work is more important to you—because you hate it that much or because you're trying to prove some sort of point—than your partner's happiness, it might be time to take a hard look at that relationship, because when someone else's happiness is important to you, sometimes their priorities need to become priorities for you, too.

WHETHER YOU'RE BOUND to the people you live with by blood, choice, or just a pressing need to be able to pay the rent, it's in everyone's best interest to try to find a fair and equitable solution to the housework problem. Harmony in cohabitation can be achieved with a little bit of compromise from everyone involved, even if it means sometimes doing stuff you really don't want to do. When you're not constantly annoyed by housework battles, you might find you actually like the person you're sharing space with.

ASKING FOR HELP OR HELPING SOMEONE ELSE

The last thing you want to do when you feel like your house is a total shithole is invite someone into it. If it's bad enough that your place looks like a tornado hit it, why on earth would you want to compound the problem by having someone witness it in all of its horrifying glory? Why would you want to give people the opportunity to judge and mock you, right? Well, kind of, but not really. Those thoughts are valid, but there's another side to it.

One of the weird and cool things about human nature is that we generally despise dealing with our own messes, but lots of us absolutely love getting our hands on someone else's. A mess we create ourselves is usually mortifying and shameful, but someone else's mess is like a brand-new episode of a home makeover show, and we want to be the star, not the subject. There's a reason that "before" and "after" pictures are so deeply satisfying. It speaks to that part of us that sees a problem and immediately starts thinking about how to fix it. Even better that it's not actually our problem to solve.

And then there are the emotional associations. When you look at your own mess, your feelings are most likely negative: disappointment, failure, helplessness, shame. When you come into someone else's space for the express purpose of helping to clean it up, you're a superhero. You're helpful and considerate and acting with that person's best interests in mind. See the difference? Granted, these emotions don't always make a ton of sense, as emotions are so rarely logical, but they're really pretty common. Helping is awesome! Being helped . . . less awesome, at least in our minds. And that association tends to prevent us from utilizing all of the tools at our disposal.

So while we're often embarrassed by the state of our homes, we might be missing out on a valuable resource for helping us get things straightened out: our friends and family. In healthy relationships, these people want us to be happy, and they understand that our homes might get a little out of hand. Of course, unhealthy relationships can be full of judgment and short on understanding on both sides, so throwing two people who feel that way into a messy space in order to clean it up can be a recipe for disaster. If you feel like someone is going to be shitty about it or use it against you, don't ask them, even if they're the tidiest, most organized person you know. (Maybe especially then. Organization without empathy can be a dangerous combination; just ask that really horrible boss you had that one time.) But if you have someone who's looking out for you, they might be your best bet for helping wrangle your mess if you can come around to feeling comfortable asking for their help.

Don't misunderstand; there's a lot of trust involved in allowing someone into your space to help you get things under control. You have to trust them to be kind, supportive, and honest. But if you have someone like that in your life it's a huge asset and a resource you should be taking advantage of. Someone in your life who's expressed concern or offered help in the past might be just the person to help you out, as long as the concern comes in the form of support, not criticism. You might have people in your life who would love to help you out but don't know how to broach the subject, or don't want to hurt your feelings. Someone who's that considerate of your feelings is probably a great person to ask.

So how do you go about asking? Lots of people know that their friends and family need help with their homes, but they hesitate to overstep their boundaries by offering help. If there's someone in your life you think fits the bill, just start with a casual question. "I need to clean up around the house, and I could use an extra set of hands. Is that something you could help me with if I bribe you with pizza?" Most people are going to be pretty honest here. An enthusiastic affirmative is a green light. You might be surprised at how happy people are to be asked; so often, they're worried about you and want to help but don't know how. A gentle rejection probably just means they hate cleaning entirely, whether it's their stuff or yours. If you do get a no, try not to take it too personally. There are so many reasons someone might decline, and almost none of them have anything to do with you and everything to do with cleaning in general.

Once you've rallied some help with wrangling your mess, here are some tips for making the most of it.

PREPLANNING

Before your help arrives, sit down and figure out what *you* need to do and what you need the person who's helping you to do. Do you need your helper to make decisions about what stays and what goes, or is that the exact thing you don't want anyone else to do? Do you need a lot of help physically moving stuff around? Someone to tell you where to start and suggest what to do next? There are a million ways this can go, and it'll be most beneficial if you can figure it out beforehand. Once you decide, write down your thoughts, then sit down with the other person and talk about what you're looking for. Use your notes as a guide for the conversation, and take more notes about what arises from the discussion. They'll be pretty helpful to look back on if things get a little rocky or if you need to do a course correction partway through the process.

SOME IMPORTANT QUESTIONS FOR PREPLANNING:

- What do you want to accomplish with this big clean?
- What do you need the most help with?
- What do you want to leave for another time?
- What are you going to do with the things you get rid of?
- What do you not want your helper to do/say?

As always, honest and open communication is absolutely key here. Both sides need to be clear about what each needs from the other, and willing to stop and address concerns as they come up. The more you talk about it and establish guidelines and parameters, the smoother it'll go. You might have to get past some initial discomfort, but once you get through that, you'll be able to accomplish so much more. Having a clearly defined plan, as well as talking about some of the tough things that are likely to come up while you're working, will be incredibly useful. This can be awkward to talk about, but if you've gotten to the point where you're willing to have someone in your home to help you clean it up, and that someone has agreed to do it, you're both already on board.

There's a lot in this process that has the potential to be emotional or difficult. There's so much fear involved: fear of asking for help, fear of dealing with your mess, fear of judgment, fear of what might be lurking inside that invisible corner. There's no avoiding it. So the best thing you can do is to get it out in the open. If you know that sorting through your closet is going to be hard for you, say so. If you're dreading having to deal with shredding years' worth of old bills, bring that up. Your helper might have ideas of ways to work through it, and if not, at the very least they'll know you might need some extra care. Make no mistake, the planning is just as important as the actual cleaning and organizing. Going in haphazardly is a pretty surefire way for things to get complicated and messed up when you're in the middle of it. Don't skimp on the planning. It might also have the bonus effect of making you feel calmer and more confident overall about the whole thing.

DURING THE PROCESS

It might be hard to start. It might even be hard to open the door and let your helper in. The fear of judgment and all of the negative emotions you're carrying about the state of your home are likely to make it very difficult to get going. Just remember that this person is here for you. You've been open and honest with them, and they've been honest right back, and they want to help.

Things aren't going to go exactly as planned. It might even get difficult and crappy and frustrating. Everyone involved is going to get mad, or upset, or overwhelmed. That's all totally OK. You know that it's going to happen going into it, so just be prepared. If you came up with a game plan early on (like I told you to), that's great. You can follow the steps you laid out and move past whatever the problem is. Let's be real, though. You probably didn't do that. You got excited about the project and couldn't wait to get started and maybe didn't plan as well as you could have. It's fine. That's human nature.

When you hit a speed bump in the process, take a step back and look at a few things. First, what's the real problem? Is it that you can't decide what to do with that hideous sweater your favorite aunt gave you, or are you afraid if you get rid of the sweater it'll somehow be a commentary on your relationship with Auntie Barbara? Once you can figure out what's really bothering you, it might be a little bit easier for you to work through.

Next, ask yourself what you want the result of the current problem to be and, more importantly, what you're *afraid* it will be. As I mentioned earlier, fear is behind so much of this process. Whether it's fear of a drastic change in your surroundings, or losing the comfort of having all of your possessions out and available for mental inventory, there's definitely some freak-out feelings in there somewhere. Acknowledge it, name it if you need to, and figure out why it's tripping you up. If your helper is someone who can be emotionally supportive on this level, take advantage of that! Use their support to help you work through it.

As you're working, **take breaks.** Make sure you're fed and hydrated and not overexerting yourself. Check in and see how you're doing emotionally. Let yourself have a good cry if you need one, or a ridiculous dance party to shake off some nervous energy. Have a corny funeral for your discarded possessions. (Just maybe not a Viking funeral; we don't need to get fire involved with all this hard work and emotion.) Take pictures! Not just "befores" and "afters," although those are pretty important, but also pictures of things you might be reluctant to get rid of, or just progress pictures so you can look back and see what you accomplished at various stages in the process. Photodocumenting the process is a great way to give yourself a little bit of distance from all of the difficult stuff you're working through, and it turns the whole process into more of an anthropological study and less of a self-criticism.

AFTERWARD

Follow-up is key, for everyone involved. If it's your home that got cleaned up, you need to make an effort to make sure it doesn't get back to that "before" stage. Use the resources you've acquired and do what you can to keep on top of your home and your mess. Make sure you're doing something—anything—every day that's a positive interaction with your living environment. Clear off your coffee table and put some flowers in a vase. Hang up your clothes and put on your favorite sweater. Wash your dishes and make a mug of gourmet hot cocoa. That'll help keep you from backsliding and also ensure you're feeling pretty good about where you live and how much work you've done to make it awesome.

There might be some emotional stuff to deal with after a major overhaul. You'll probably feel a lot of relief and pride once you're all done, but you might also feel some other things you aren't totally prepared for. Perhaps loss for the stuff you got rid of. Or a little shame that it took so long to start undoing the mess.

It's natural to have these feelings, but don't let yourself wallow in them. Sure, you might feel guilty that you let it get "that" bad, but you should also feel a pretty significant amount of satisfaction and accomplishment that you did all of the difficult things involved in fixing it.

If you're the person who helped, don't just finish the project and forget about it. Your friend is going to need some support for a while. Maybe some reassurance that they did the right thing, maybe some ongoing help to keep from getting overwhelmed, or maybe just someone to talk to. A major overhaul of one's living space can be a lot to take in all at once, and the aftermath can be a little tricky. Be there for your friend as much as you can, and lend support however it's needed.

With cooperation and communication at every stage in the process, you can make a huge difference in the condition of your (or someone else's) living space. Just remember to stay open and honest, check in frequently, and stay positive, focused, and nonjudgmental.

And see the Conversation Start-up Kit in the Resources section for some suggested things to say before, during, and after the cleanup.

What to do if you're the helper

If you have a friend whose home is a mess and you want to help, you need to tread carefully. (This goes double if it's a family member.) It's very easy to hurt someone's feelings or make them feel self-conscious or embarrassed about this. Once they ask for your help, be positive, be supportive, and keep their feelings in mind. For example:

Not helpful. "Oh, thank God you're finally doing something about that trash heap!"

Helpful. "I'm so glad you felt comfortable asking me. I'd love to help! What can I do?"

See the difference?

The very act of asking for help is fraught with emotion and fear. Don't make it worse. Keep in mind that every word and action from you, especially in the beginning, will set the tone for how this goes. Choose your words and actions carefully and with the knowledge that the person who asked you for help is likely feeling pretty vulnerable and exposed right now. If you're positive and supportive, that fear and vulnerability will start to go away. If you're negative, critical, or judgmental, your friend is soon going to regret asking, and the whole process will be more difficult for everyone (mostly the asker). If you don't think you can be sensitive, sympathetic, and constructive, it might be better to gently decline the request for help rather than risk irreparably damaging your relationship. If you do say no, do it kindly and without judgment; if you can give a solid, easy-to-understand reason that has nothing to do with the person, do so. It'll go a long way toward avoiding feelings of rejection.

If you are willing to be part of the process, being the helper can be tricky. You need to find a good balance between being useful and respecting the rules and limitations of the person you're helping. You might want to completely empty the place out, tossing trash and unneeded possessions indiscriminately. That might be what the space needs, but it probably isn't what your friend needs. They might only be ready to tackle the obvious trash and the dishes. They might not be prepared to sort through and decide the fate of all of their possessions, so don't push it. Just do what they ask you to. Unless you've been given the authority, don't start chucking stuff out left and right. You want your friend to be open to more help in the future, and the best way to do that is to not push for more than they're ready to do.

You can certainly offer suggestions, but take no for an answer the first time and get back on track as quickly and easily as you can.

In case you were wondering, yes, it's 100 percent possible to do more harm than good; for example, by taking liberties with your friend's space or getting rid of things you weren't supposed to. Just because it seems obvious to you that something needs to get chucked doesn't mean it's OK for you to make that decision. Think of yourself as a set of hands controlled by someone else's brain. You're not here to make the decisions; you're here to help the person who made the decisions do the work. If all has gone well in the early stages of this big clean, you'll have had an open and frank discussion of what's going to happen, how it's all going to go down, and what you can and can't do to help.

Here are a few more things to keep in mind as the helper:

- **DON'T OVERSTEP.** Do what you've been asked, but don't take initiative that you haven't been given. You might think every single thing in a room needs to be thrown out, but if the person who owns those things doesn't agree, you don't have the right to override them unless they've given you permission beforehand.

- **BE PATIENT.** This can be hard, but an impatient or overly critical helper can derail the entire process.

- **BE SUPPORTIVE.** Your friend may only be able or willing to do small amounts, and that's fine. Let them know you're there to support them, whatever they decide to do.

- **BE POSITIVE!** This process is really difficult for the person you're helping, and they can use as much optimism about the whole thing as you can give them. Positively reinforce their decisions, no matter how obvious they might seem, to help remove some of the hesitancy they might be feeling.

- **DON'T IMPOSE YOUR OWN STANDARDS.** You might look around when you're nearly done and think it's still pretty terrible. You can think that, sure, but keep it to yourself. You're not the person whose opinion matters. You need to defer to the person you're helping to get to the level of clean or organized that they're comfortable with.

- **DON'T JUDGE.** If ever there was a time to keep your negative opinions to yourself, this is it. Keep in mind that your words are pretty powerful here, and you can end up being incredibly hurtful even if you don't mean to. Think carefully about what comes out of your mouth. If you can't keep from making negative or judgmental comments, you might not be actually helping at all.

- **TAKE NO FOR AN ANSWER.** Once again, remember that you're not steering this ship. If you think you know the best way to handle something, but the person you're helping doesn't agree, it's not your place to try to override their decision. Accept "no" gracefully and with the understanding that it's not about you at all.

4

SPECIAL CASES

Emergency Unfucking

Moving

Unfucking Your Digital Life

Schoolwork and Work Work

EMERGENCY UNFUCKING

The phone rings. It's your mom, or your landlord, or an old friend who's in town and wants to stop in. You hang up the phone and realize that you have to get your home ready for the presence of another human being within a day or less. That's . . . terrifying. You look around your house and realize that you haven't picked anything up in weeks (or months; no one's judging you here!), and it dawns on you that there's no way to turn it into something that looks like an actual responsible adult lives in it within a reasonable amount of time. So the panic sets in, and you start trying to think of a way, any way, to keep other people out of your space so you can avoid having to deal with it right now. But resist the urge to panic. Panic leads to fear, fear leads to procrastination, and procrastination leads to the dark side, the dark side being where you lock the doors, close the blinds, and hope whoever's coming over just forgets the whole thing and leaves you alone.

While that's a perfectly understandable response, it's not particularly helpful when, for example, your landlord gives you notice of an inspection, or your heat is broken and you need to let the repairperson come in and do their thing so you don't freeze to death. In some circumstances, you really just have to let someone in. There's no way around it. So now it's time to turn your panic into something useful and channel all of that stress into getting things well enough in order so that you won't be embarrassed or evicted. It seems pretty hopeless, I know, but you can make it better. You just need to turn your disaster of a place into somewhere you can actually let people into. Remember, panic is not your friend, so make peace with the fact that someone is going to be in your space, and get ready to go to work.

Emergency cleaning is a special circumstance, outside of the scope of what we're trying to accomplish long-term in regard to cleaning and organizing. You're looking to bring the overall state of things to a point where someone can come in and look around; hell, maybe even sit down and stay a while! (OK, let's not go overboard.) You're going to be focusing on pretty much everything, and you need to make sure you aren't getting distracted by side projects or spending time on areas that aren't going to make much difference in the grand scheme of your home's overall cleanliness.

The time for procrastination is done, and it's time to get to it. Your time here is limited, you're working on a deadline, and you can't put it off any longer. While sitting around stressing about it is completely normal, it's not something that's helping you to get things ready. So acknowledge that this whole process is pretty crappy and stressful and that you're going to be working your ass off for a little while, then move that to the back burner long enough to buckle down and get some shit done. Eventually, the goal is to get you to a place where your base level of clean is good enough that emergency cleaning is no longer necessary. But if you aren't at that point yet, having a solid plan in place is necessary to avoid the panic inherent in these situations. The clearer your plan, the easier it will be to follow, and the less likely you are to give up or get overwhelmed.

When you're emergency cleaning, you can't be focusing on the tiny little details. You're looking to bring the general mess level down from a 10 to a 5 or 4 or wherever you can get it in the time that you have. If you're not looking at the big picture, you're going to end up with a couple of really sparkling clean spots in the middle of a disaster area. Think of it like sanding a really rough piece of wood. If you concentrate on just sanding one tiny spot, you're going to end up with one very smooth spot surrounded by a whole lot of rough patches, whereas if you just do a little across the whole surface, the whole thing is going to be smoother overall. It might not be perfect, but it's better, and it's all about the same level, so nothing looks comparatively better or worse than any other part. So keep your attention on making the mess better overall, rather than trying to deep-clean every square inch to perfection.

As you're emergency cleaning, you're probably going to get distracted by things you notice that need attention, and it's going to seem like now would be a great time to do this stuff. It's not. You're going to be tempted to start a detailed project—maybe organize your bookshelf or clean out the fridge or finally cull your sock collection. Don't. Now is not the time for that. That'll eat up a big chunk of time that you just don't have. If it makes you feel better, keep a list of the projects you're tempted to start. You can always revisit them once you're past this crisis, but do not make the mistake of wasting time on detailed stuff that's not going to make a noticeable difference in the overall level of mess. You need to get started, and you need to do it now.

GET READY

First things first: You need to get prepared for what's ahead. Put on some great music or your favorite podcast, eat something, and make sure your beverage of choice is close at hand. (Not an alcoholic one. Drunk cleaning is like an advanced class, and you're not at that stage yet. You can't afford to lose time on an ill-placed nap or a drunken debate on the hierarchy of '90s pop stars and their discographies.) Put the computer away unless you're using it for music. You don't need to get distracted with the Internet and risk losing your momentum. **Do not fool yourself into thinking you can "just check something online real quick" and then you'll get right back to work.** You won't, and you know it. It's too easy to lose huge chunks of time online and then look up hours later and wonder where the day went. Distractions of all kinds, whether it's a detailed household project or an Internet spiral, are the enemy here, and they're what's most likely to keep you from getting everything done. As you take your breaks throughout the emergency cleaning process, consider whether or not spending them online is a good idea for you. If you in any way doubt your ability to walk away from the computer after ten minutes, it's better to just avoid it all together until you're done.

Once you're prepared, **make your bed.** Yeah, I know. You hate making your bed, and it seems like this should not be the priority right now. But this will give you someplace tidy to retreat to if necessary, and will immediately make your bedroom look, like, 20 percent cleaner with the bare minimum of effort. Next, **get your cleaning supplies together.** Make sure you have plenty of trash bags and some dust rags. Locate your vacuum cleaner and a broom. Take a minute and **fill the kitchen sink up with some hot soapy water** so you can put dirty dishes in there as you go. (If there are already dishes in it, that's fine! This will only help you out later on.) Fill the bathroom sink with some soapy water, too. It'll help make everything easier to clean later. **Open the shades or curtains,** and if it's possible, open the windows to get some fresh air circulating.

GET GOING

Now it's time to really get started. Grab a trash bag and go from room to room to **throw away anything that's obviously trash.** Pick up any recyclables and make sure those get to where they need to go, too. Work methodically around each room, starting from the entrance, working in one direction, and looking up, down, and around. Once you've finished collecting all of the trash you can find, take the bags out of your house if that's possible. Keep in mind that putting things like trash bags *down* instead of taking them *out* means you're just going to have to deal with them later. Save yourself the time and aggravation by doing it all at once. While you're at it, collect the trash from any other cans or bags you have elsewhere and take that out, too. Replace the trash bags in the cans, if applicable. With just the trash taken care of, it's probably already looking (and smelling) a little bit better. Take a minute to breathe and relax a little bit; it's all going to get done, and it's going to be OK.

Next, go from room to room and **gather up all the dishes.**

Go ahead and deposit them in that sink full of soapy water you set up before you got started. If the sink is already full, wash one load of dishes or load up the dishwasher. Get another load of things soaking and then move on. Once you move on to the rest of the house, after each stage, revisit the dishes and do some more. Don't get totally wrapped up in dishes, though; you want to be doing other stuff in between. If your dish situation is bad enough, you could theoretically spend all day on it, and that's not what we're aiming for here. Once the first phase of dish warfare is over, take a ten-minute break and grab a bite to eat or something to drink and recharge a little. But most importantly, when your break is over, you need to get up and get moving again.

Postbreak, do another round to every room and **get all your stray clothes together.** Clean laundry needs to get put away in its proper home, and dirty laundry needs to go in the hamper (or whatever it is you're using in lieu of a hamper). You don't need to start a load, but just make sure it's all together in the right place, so no one is going to stumble over your dirty socks (or worse . . .) when they're least expecting it. That just gets embarrassing for both of you. If you have a little extra time, there's nothing wrong with throwing some clothes in the washer, but keep in mind that laundry has three steps, and if you aren't going to be able to (or want to) put it away, then just go ahead and save the laundry for later. The important thing is to get it off of the floor and the furniture. You don't need to share your floor-drobe with the world, or even your landlord.

Once your garbage, dishes, and laundry are under control, think about where people are going to actually be when they're in your house. If it's a social visit, they're probably not going to end up in the bedroom (unless it's, you know, a *social* visit), so you can probably just shut that door and not worry about it too much beyond trash, dishes, and laundry. This tactic doesn't work if, for example, your landlord is coming over for maintenance and will need to get in there, or if you're not totally sure where they're going to need access. Regardless, even if you're closing off doors, it's still good to have the trash and dishes dealt with. As far as closets and cabinets, unless you have reason to believe that someone's going to be opening these, leave them alone. Don't give in to the temptation to put more crap in them—because you're just going to have to deal with it later—but don't make them a cleaning or organizing priority right now. You can do it once the visit is over.

In the visible areas like the kitchen and living room, clearing off your flat surfaces is going to go a very long way toward making the place look a lot less chaotic, even if it's not particularly clean. Things tend to accumulate on anything horizontal, so a huge amount of your clutter is likely concentrated on those surfaces. **Start with the most visible flat surfaces (tables, countertops, etc.) and clear them off.** Do your best not to simply relocate the contents to somewhere else that you're just going to have to deal with later—baskets and boxes full of random junk rarely get put away, and you know it—but try instead to put things away for good. It's tempting to just stash all the crap behind one of those doors you closed before, but all you're doing when you do that is shifting the mess; you're not actually cleaning up. In the absolute worst of time crunches, this is an OK, if not ideal, way to deal with things, but if there's any possible way to avoid it, do. **Don't just stash the junk somewhere else. Put it away.** Otherwise, months from now, you're going to find yourself tripping over those baskets of random crap you stashed in a hurry, and you'll be right back where you started for the next unexpected visit.

Keep working on your counters, tables, and shelves until

they're all passably clear. Once you've cleared one off, wipe it down. After finishing one surface, go do some more dishes before moving on to the next area. Take a short break every so often. It might seem counterintuitive to take a break when you're dealing with such strict time constraints, but it'll help to keep you from getting burned out and grumpy. Chances are, grumpy is going to show up anyway, but that's OK. All that intense work on a deadline is basically a recipe for crankiness, to which very few of us are immune. **Take some time to regroup and do something nice for yourself.** Flat surfaces are probably going to take up the bulk of your time, so pace yourself as best you can while still working quickly and efficiently and avoiding distractions.

After your flat surfaces are clear, **do a quick dusting** of anything you haven't gotten to, if needed. Don't spend a lot of time on this; just do a quick wipe-down of anything that's obviously dusty and gross. Half-assing the job is totally acceptable here since we're going for speed. No need to go all out trying to do it perfectly. A quick go-through with glass cleaner for any visible glass is good. Get the bathroom mirror, too, while you're at it. **Don't even think about trying to wash your windows,** though. Windows take forever, and some things will just have to wait.

Now, especially if you're expecting a social visit, **spend some time cleaning up in the bathroom.** If it's a maintenance or landlord visit and the problem isn't in the bathroom, just do the bare minimum: Put things away, wipe down the counters and toilet, and sweep. If you're having people over who are likely to need to use the bathroom at some point, be a little bit more thorough. Bathroom time is alone time, and in someone else's house, people notice things because there's really nothing else to look at. So take a few minutes and wipe everything down, give the toilet a good cleaning, change out the hand towels, and make sure you're all stocked up on soap and toilet paper. Take a break when you're done.

Next, move into the kitchen. Your dishes should be pretty well dealt with at this point, so just put away any remaining clean ones. Your counters should be fairly clear after having been cleaned off with the other flat surfaces, so now take a few minutes to **wipe down the stove** and any grungy surfaces like cabinets or the outside of the microwave, and put away anything else that's not where it belongs. Wipe down the counters and do one last sweep of dishes to make sure the sink is (finally) clear. If there's more trash to take out, now would be a good time to handle that. Don't forget to take another little break!

DOUBLE-CHECK

If you're expecting your landlord or a maintenance call, go to wherever they're going to be working or inspecting, and take a couple of minutes to clean up that spot. If their attention is going to be focused on a fairly small area, it might be a good idea to tidy it up a little more thoroughly. Also, if you know from a previous inspection that there's something your landlord is particularly fixated on, spend some time on that. In general, landlords like to make sure the appliances are in good shape and that everything is basically clean and in good condition. Structural issues are the landlord's responsibility (whether or not they actually accept that responsibility varies greatly), but cosmetic appearance and overall cleanliness are your job, and that's what the landlord is going to be looking at. So take a few minutes to do a little more work on that.

Once that's done, take another lap around to every room and deal with anything that's jumping out at you as out of place or messy. If you notice it, another person might, too. Again, don't get too wrapped up in any one thing; you're not looking to do a deep clean, just taking the overall mess down a notch. Once you're happy, or at least content, with the general state of things, clean up the floors. **Run a vacuum or do a quick sweep,** but unless it's totally necessary, you can skip a thorough mopping. If anything is sticky or gross, do a basic mop with some hot water, but don't get all wrapped up in getting your floors clean enough to eat off of. No one's actually going to eat off your floor (I'm hoping?), so that's just going to take up a chunk of time you really don't have to spare. Again, you're looking for improvement, not perfection, so do the best you can quickly, and then make sure you put all of your cleaning supplies away once you've finished.

Once you're done, step outside of your home (be very careful not to lock yourself out!) and walk back in. If anything catches your eye or is out of place, deal with it quickly. Once that's done, high-five yourself on a job well done. (I guess this looks sort of like a clap?) Take a shower, put on some clean clothes, and have something to eat. Emergency cleaning is stressful and crappy, and you got through it! Now try to enjoy having other people in your home, knowing that all your hard work means they might just be fooled into thinking you have your shit together.

MOVING

Y ou're moving! That's so great! Oh, wait, no. It's the other thing. Terrible. Moving is absolutely terrible, and everyone who does it swears they'll never do it again—until they do. It's exhausting, tedious, frustrating, and basically the worst. It's awful, and everyone knows it. It doesn't have to be, though. You can move without it being the worst, most stressful thing you can experience. It can be relatively painless if you're well prepared and well organized. And you can be. Starting out smart and staying on track will bring the pain level of moving down from "wild jaguar attack" to "mildly inconvenient mosquito bite." It's still going to suck, but with some preparation and organization, you can make it suck a little less.

The most useful thing you can do to keep from going completely bananas is to start early. Even if your move seems like it's ages away, you should start preparing as soon as you know the move is happening. This gives you the time you need to pack more intelligently, stay organized, and, most importantly, keep yourself sane in the process. Moving doesn't have to be as stressful as it's been in the past. Procrastinating until the last minute, though, is a surefire way to end up crying in your kitchen, surrounded by things shoved in garbage bags and a moving truck idling outside. Don't let yourself get to this stage. Start early. And if you can't start early, start now. Even one extra day of preparation can help (although obviously, more is better if you have the time).

STAGE 1: MONTHS/WEEKS IN ADVANCE

Starting off on the right foot will save you a lot of time and aggravation later on. While this stage is almost entirely preparation, it's still really important in the grand scheme of things and will pave the way for more intense packing when you're ready for that. Starting early gives you the opportunity to do a little less work at a time and to avoid getting burned out.

- **START CULLING.** This is the single most important thing you can do to make your move easier. Don't move things you don't want to keep. Don't move things that will eventually become garbage. *Do not move anything you know you will not want or use once you move.* If you think you're going to be discarding a lot of stuff or large items you can't donate, now's the time to arrange for a Dumpster or recycling pickup. Now is the time to really go through and figure out which of your possessions aren't necessary or wanted. It's silly to move things only to end up getting rid of them once you're moved.

- **SET UP REGULAR PICKUPS OR DROP-OFFS.** Many nonprofits have collection trucks for donated items, which makes it a lot easier for you to get things you don't want out of your house. A quick online search can help you find organizations that will pick up donations locally. Once you've decided to get rid of something, move it to a specific area, and make sure you move it out as soon as you can. If no pickup service is available where you are, designate a day to go drop off donations; if you have a lot of stuff, schedule a drop-off every week, or whatever interval is appropriate for you.

- **DESIGNATE A STAGING AREA.** When you get into the full swing of packing, you're going to want a system for dealing with your boxes that makes sense. Once boxes get filled up, you should have a designated place to put them so that they're ready to move without being in the way. Now is the time to set that space up. Prep the area by clearing other things out of it—make sure you can work around it as you're packing!—and just generally getting it ready to hold your boxes.

- **DO SOMETHING EVERY SINGLE DAY.** This UfYH mantra works for moving, too. Even if your move is pretty far away, make it a point to work on one area or pack one box a day. When you start skipping days, it makes it that much harder to get back into the swing of things, and you'll find yourself with a lot of lost time to make up for. Keep a slow and steady pace, and don't be lulled into complacency by how far away your move is. That time is going to fly by, so make sure it's productive.

- **DEAL WITH YOUR BAGGAGE.** If you happen to have boxes that you never unpacked from a previous move (don't worry, everyone does), now's the time to finally deal with them. I mean, come on, if you haven't opened or unpacked something in however long you've been living where you are, is it something you really need to be hanging on to? Open that box and decide once and for all if you're keeping the stuff or tossing it. Bonus, if tossing: You now have an empty box to use for packing and a bunch less stuff to move!

STAGE 2: A FEW WEEKS AWAY TO RIGHT BEFORE

As the move looms closer, you can start to prepare more intensely. By this point, you'll (hopefully) have gotten rid of anything you don't want to move with you, so you're ready to start packing for real. As always, starting out organized is going to pay off later, so take a little bit of this time to set up your systems in advance. It'll keep you on track as things start getting chaotic. At this stage, you don't have a lot of extra time to mess around with, so buckle down and commit to accomplishing a set amount every day to keep the last few days from being more than you can handle.

- **STOCK UP ON YOUR SUPPLIES.** You're going to need boxes, obviously, but also make sure you have plenty of packing tape, garbage bags, paper for wrapping up breakables, and markers. You don't want to interrupt your packing flow by having to run to the store. Put all of your packing supplies in one easy-to-access place, and when you've finished working for the day, put everything back in that spot. Don't waste valuable time by having to chase down your packing tape or wondering where you left the marker.

- **WORK METHODICALLY.** Start with things you use infrequently, or that you know you won't need until after you move. Work around your home in a logical order so you aren't going back to the same area time and again. It may not be possible to finish a room entirely, especially if there are still things in that room that you need before the move, but do as much as you can before moving on to somewhere else, or consolidate the things you need into one area.

- **ONLY HANDLE EACH AREA ONCE.** Pick one drawer, shelf, square foot of floor space, or cabinet at a time. Deal with every single item in that space, whether you get rid of it or pack it. Once the space is done, clean it out. If it's a fixture that stays in the old place, you're saving yourself some time cleaning it off later, and if it's something that's moving with you, it's much nicer to unpack clean things. Going back to the same area over and over will waste your time and keep you from getting through the process quickly and efficiently. Doing one at a time also helps you stay organized, because you won't be constantly wondering if you left something behind in an area you've already worked on.

- **TAKE BREAKS!** The great thing about starting early is that it gives you a little more time to work with, and you can hopefully avoid burning yourself out. If you didn't start early, breaks are just as important to avoid becoming a giant stress monster. Moving is a stressful process no matter what, so put some effort into trying to mitigate some of that tension. Either set a timer, or enforce breaks after one or two areas. If you start to feel like packing is all that you're doing, you're going to be even more unhappy than this process already makes you. Schedule in some time away from packing, and give yourself rewards for getting things done. The process sucks, there's no getting around that, but it's so much worse if it's dominating all of your time.

- **LABEL EVERYTHING.** Everyone in the universe has advice on how to label packing boxes, but you need to know what's going to work for you. The most common advice seems to be to color-code everything, with a master list of contents that corresponds with each box. That is some next-level organizing skill that most of us don't possess, and it can be fairly time-consuming and confusing if you're not naturally inclined to it. Try just writing the contents on the box, and be specific. Rather than "Kitchen," use your marker to scrawl out "Kitchen: wine glasses, gadget drawer, serving platters." Future You will thank Past You for being so thorough, and it doesn't require a master's degree in organization.

- **DON'T MOVE BOXES MORE OFTEN THAN YOU HAVE TO.** Remember the staging area you set up in stage 1? Here's where it comes in handy. Once your box is packed up and labeled, seal it and take it to the staging area. The next time you touch it should be when you're loading it up to move. If possible, try to group boxes in the staging area based on where they're going to go in the new place. That'll help when you're unpacking the truck on moving day.

- **PACK UP ALL BUT THE BARE NECESSITIES.** You don't have to wait until the day before you move to pack your dishes and utensils and such. Separate one set of daily items for each person who lives in the house and pack everything else. When it's time to move, all that stuff can go in one box, and you can start using it right away in the new place. Everything else can get dealt with and packed up. Keep in mind, too, that you'll probably be able to make do in the short term without a whole lot of things you may currently consider necessities. If you can do without it for a little while, pack it up.

- **MAKE A LIST OF IMMEDIATE NEEDS.** Figure out what you're going to need in the first twenty-four to forty-eight hours in the new place and make a list. As close as possible to moving day, pack a box with all of those things and label it clearly so that it's easily accessible once you've moved. Consider not just the obvious things like bedding, dishes, and clothes but also things like a shower curtain, your medication, pet food, cleaning supplies for the new place, and anything else you'll need to establish your daily routine once you're in your new abode. Make a mental inventory of those essential items as you go through your daily routine in the time leading up to the move so you aren't scrambling at the last minute to figure out what you're going to need.

- **STAY ON TRACK.** Resist the urge to throw everything into unlabeled garbage bags. It may be easier now, but it's not going to help once you've moved and it's time to unpack. If you are using garbage bags for soft goods (pillows, clothes, sheets), make sure the bags are labeled so they don't get mistaken for trash and end up in the Dumpster. Even better, try to find clear bags so you can see at a glance what's inside. Avoid accidentally throwing out your possessions by taking trash out as soon as the bag is full.

- **MAKE A PLAN FOR THE LITTLE ONES.** If you have pets or kids, consider making alternate arrangements for them for moving day. It's hard enough to stay on task as it is, and worrying about leaving the door open or whether it's naptime will only add to your stress.

STAGE 3: MOVING DAY

It's time! Moving day can be chaotic and complicated, but if you've planned well and stayed on track up to this point, things should go fairly smoothly. Plan for at least a few things to go horribly wrong, though, so you aren't too surprised when they inevitably do. Try to be well rested so you're better equipped to handle whatever comes up. Eat a good breakfast, stay hydrated, play some music if you can, and try to stay relaxed.

- **ENLIST HELP.** This may go without saying, but the more hands to help, the better. Every additional helper cuts your loading and unloading time dramatically, and relieves the pressure on you to do everything yourself. The time-honored tradition of bribing your friends and family with pizza and beer is helpful (as is any food, really), but also helpful is reciprocity. Always remember the people who helped you move. You owe them.

- **PUT EACH BOX WHERE IT BELONGS.** Since you were awesome and organized while packing, you know where each box's contents belong. Make sure that's where they end up. There's no sense in bringing a box into the house, putting it down somewhere, and then, at some later time, having to pick it back up and move it somewhere else before you can put its contents away. Just take it right where it belongs.

- **TAKE A TIME-OUT!** You're going to want to get as much done as quickly as possible, and while that's definitely important, it's also important to give everyone short periods to rest and recharge. In addition, remember to eat, stay hydrated, and stay on schedule with any medications you take. When you're in the midst of a big move, your routines can get all screwed up, so make sure you remember the important stuff.

- **CLEAN THE OLD PLACE.** I get it, you can't wait to be done with the place, but leaving it clean and in good condition will minimize aggravation and increase the likelihood of getting your whole security deposit back. If you remembered to clean as you were packing, this step shouldn't be too terrible. If it's really horrible, consider hiring someone to clean, or see if one of your moving helpers would be willing to clean instead of hauling boxes.

- **REGROUP.** When things go wrong—and they probably will, to some extent—don't panic. Figure out the quickest and easiest way to address the problem, or delegate as necessary, and then get back to work. Some things will happen that are beyond your control: A broken-down moving truck is a sadly common thing that can wreck your whole move if you don't have a contingency plan, so make sure all of your details are clarified and you have a backup plan just in case things go south.

STAGE 4: UNPACKING

Once you're all moved in and surrounded by a fort of boxes, it's time to start the unpacking process. The sooner you get it finished, the sooner you can relax and actually enjoy your new place without all that work hanging over your head.

- **UNPACK THOROUGHLY AND METHODICALLY.** The last thing you need is to have things lingering in boxes months after you move. Empty a box, break the box down and stash it away, and move on to the next one. Leaving half-filled boxes isn't ideal, not only because you have to handle the same box more than once, but also because your overall number of boxes isn't going to decrease as you work. Your goal should be to clear out the boxes and get the contents put away properly as quickly as you can.

- **START OUT ORGANIZED.** Designate a space for packing materials once you start unpacking, and make sure you're regularly taking them out to be recycled so the moving detritus doesn't take over your new place. Make sure everything stays in whatever place you've designated, and reset each area to clean once you're done unpacking for the moment.

- **WORK EVERY DAY.** Again, as with packing, aim for at least a few boxes or twenty minutes every day. If you get out of the habit of steadily unpacking, you'll find it that much more difficult to get started again. Slow, steady, and only mildly annoyed wins the race here. You still need to live your actual life amid all of the unpacking, so do a little bit each day and then move on to something else until tomorrow.

- **STEP AWAY FOR A MINUTE.** Unpacking can be as exhausting as packing. If you try to do too much and burn yourself out, you're not doing yourself any favors, and you're much more likely to give up partway through and leave boxes untouched and sitting around until the next time you have to do this all over again. Especially in the beginning, when you're likely to be dealing with a number of boxes at the same time, take a breather every once in a while.

A new home is the perfect opportunity to start fresh with a clean, organized space. As you're unpacking, try to consider what setup is going to help keep you on an orderly path. Starting from scratch is sometimes much easier than trying to get an established mess under control. You have the chance to set things up any way you want, so put some thought into how to organize your new space in a way that works for you.

UNFUCKING YOUR DIGITAL HABITAT

These days, we exist in digital space almost as much as we do IRL (that's "in real life" for you nonliners). Your digital habitat is just as important and just as vulnerable to unholy disasters as your physical one. Whether it's your mess of an email inbox, your improbably large number of Facebook "friends," or your impossible-to-search Documents and Pictures folders, your digital life can probably use a little unfucking.

The same principles that we've been using to deal with our physical messes can be applied to our digital messes: working in small bursts, taking breaks, and doing a little bit of prevention on a daily basis. Going through and organizing an entire inbox or all of your computer's documents can be a huge task, so tackle it one manageable chunk at a time. Whether that means setting a timer or putting a limit on how many messages or files you deal with at a time, breaking this job down into smaller sections will keep it from taking over your life. Sure, it may take days to get everything back down to something manageable, but having a plan and a deadline will help, even if it doesn't all get done at once. Which it probably won't.

EMAIL

Chances are, your inbox is a mess of unread messages, junk mail, and a seemingly infinite backlog of stuff you really don't need to hang on to. With a little effort, you can wrangle your messages into something far more manageable and less dismaying.

- **SORT BY SENDER.** You can delete wide swaths of emails this way if you know they're coming from a sender you don't care about. Store sales and promotions, that newsletter you got automatically subscribed to, your aunt who only ever sends you forwarded hoaxes and "feel-good" stories—you can make them all go away at once (the emails, not your technologically challenged family members). Plus, emails from the same sender will often be sorted into the same category, which will make filing them much easier, too.

- **UNSUBSCRIBE.** Sorting by sender can help you identify those mailing lists you're on that are just taking up space in your inbox and have no positive value for you. Prevention is key with all kinds of mess, including digital, so reducing the number of emails coming in will help you stay organized. Just click Unsubscribe, which is usually located at the bottom of these emails.

- **MAKE LABELS.** For those things you need to hang on to, create an inbox filing system that's intuitive for you. If you need to save certain kinds of emails, create specific, easy-to-remember labels that'll make them easy for you to find later on.

- **MAINTAIN.** Don't let your unread emails creep up into the thousands. Every day, go through and sort, delete, and unsubscribe as needed. Just like with your home, a very small amount of work on a regular basis will prevent the need for a major project later on. Even if you get a hundred or more emails a day, it's considerably easier to deal with a hundred now than three thousand at the end of the month.

COMPUTER DESKTOP

Is your computer desktop a chaotic disaster of icons and short-cuts to who-knows-where? Impose some order on your desktop to make turning the computer on a little bit less stressful. A lot of people avoid the chaos of a cluttered desktop by simply never using it at all, which is absolutely a valid method, but if you're someone who still relies on your desktop as part of your computing routine, there are certainly things you can do to keep it under control.

- **DON'T USE THE DESKTOP AS FILE STORAGE.** Sure, the whole point of the desktop is for ease of access, but when it's covered by every file and folder you have, it really doesn't make anything easier to find. If there's a

file you need to access every time you use your
computer, give it a place of honor, but otherwise, use
folder storage instead.

- **KEEP CURRENT.** There is absolutely no need to keep
  things on your desktop that are out of date or unused.
  Go through and get rid of or move anything that isn't
  currently useful.

- **USE A WALLPAPER YOU LOVE.** If you have a picture that's
  meaningful to you or a pattern you're really drawn to,
  you'll be less likely to cover it in crap.

- **GET HELP.** There are lots of apps, programs, and
  extensions that offer various ways to keep your desktop
  organized. See the Resources section for some ideas.

COMPUTER FOLDERS

Admit it, you probably save all of your documents to one catch-
all Documents folder, and most of your pictures end up in one
giant Pictures folder. As I'm sure you've experienced, that can
make it a real pain in the ass to try to find something specific.
By setting up an easy-to-understand system, you'll save yourself a lot of time trying to find things later. Organization is key
here; the more streamlined and less complicated your system,
the better it'll work for you.

- **GIVE YOUR DOCUMENTS AND PICTURES NONGENERIC FILE
  NAMES.** As you save things, give them clear, descriptive
  file names that'll make them easy to locate when you're
  looking for them later. This goes for downloads of files
  you didn't create, too; you're not tied to whatever name
  (or string of numbers and letters) the creator gave

them. Rename these files to fit in with your system and keep them easy to find.

- **CREATE CATEGORIES.** Instead of Documents or Pictures, try Tax Info, Pets, Work Stuff, and so on instead. Use a system that makes sense to you, and don't be afraid to make folders within folders (2016 Receipts; Fluffy's Birthday Party; Project Research, etc.). The more levels of organization you have, the easier it'll be to find something. Sure, it takes a little longer to set up, but the work will pay off down the road.

- **CHANGE YOUR DEFAULTS.** If you like most things you save to go to one particular place, take five minutes and mess around with your settings to make that place your default. If you're more likely to look at documents you've edited recently, sort by "Date modified" rather than by name. Alphabetical order isn't always the best way to find something, despite what your third-grade teacher told you.

SOCIAL MEDIA

There's no denying that social media consumes much of our lives. Whether you're active on one social media network or five, it's easy to let it take over huge amounts of time better devoted to, you know, actually doing something. While it's certainly a great way to stay connected and informed (or misinformed, depending on what you're reading), your time on social media can probably be reduced.

- **PARE DOWN.** If spending too much time on social media is a problem for you, think about what you're relying on it for. If you're just wasting time by following a whole bunch of people you don't really care about, consider culling your friends or following list. With fewer people to follow, you'll get caught up faster and be able to get back to doing non-social-media things.

- **HIDE AND BLOCK.** When your feed or dashboard is cluttered up with irrelevant or obnoxious material, hide the source. Depending on the platform, you can often hide everything that originates from one person or one site, and in the case of a person, they'll never know that you did it. If you find yourself getting pulled into arguments or developing antagonistic relationships, don't be afraid of that "block" button. Consider what you're really getting out of those interactions, and if you don't find that the payoff is worth the aggravation, remove the source of it.

- **SCHEDULE ONLINE TIME.** Most people are fairly stunned to find out how much time they lose online. Give yourself a limit on how much consecutive time you can spend online, or use 20/10s to alternate computer time with something else you need to get done. There's nothing with wrong with catching up online, but it should be balanced with everything else that exists within your life.

SMARTPHONES

It's pretty obvious that smartphones make our lives easier in a lot of ways, but they can get disorganized and out of control just as certainly as anything else. But if you institute some order, you can find the things you use the most without getting lost in the digital clutter.

- **STREAMLINE YOUR APPS.** Make sure the apps you use most often are the most accessible on your home screen, and group everything else into folders. Name the folders something that makes sense to you. There's no need to swipe past page after page of little-used apps in order to get to what you actually need.

- **CULL YOUR CONTACTS.** Keep your contacts current and complete, and don't be afraid to delete out information for people you know you're never going to need to get in touch with again.

- **ORGANIZE YOUR PICTURES.** These days, we use our phones as cameras just as much as (or more than) we use them as phones. It's not uncommon to have thousands of pictures in your camera roll, and even though many phones separate them into albums by date, it might be useful to do a little organizing of your own. Make separate albums for trips, seasons, places, or specifically for pictures of your pets; this way you don't have to scroll through your entire archive just to find that one adorable shot of Fido frolicking at the beach.

- **BACK UP YOUR MEMORIES.** Too many people have most of their photo memories stored on their phones or hosted on their Facebook accounts with no backup. There are plenty of options available for backup and storage; just make sure you have access to yours if something were to happen to your phone (perish the thought).

Getting your digital life in order isn't always an obvious priority, especially when there's a ton of other stuff going on that seems more important, but given how much time we spend on our computers, phones, and tablets, maybe it should be. Disorganization in one area that's such a big part of our lives can lead to feeling disorganized in other ways, so no matter what environment you find yourself spending time in, whether physical or digital, it's a good idea to keep it cleaned up.

SCHOOLWORK AND WORK WORK

Think 20/10s are only useful for your house? Nope! There are all sorts of ways you can use them to accomplish a little at a time, especially school or work tasks and projects. 20/10s can be really helpful in taking a big or complex project and tackling it bit by bit. There's no end to the parts of our lives that need unfucking, but fortunately, you can use the same principles you've been applying to get your home under control to get everything else under control, too.

One of the hardest things about schoolwork (and work work) projects is finding the motivation to get started. Maybe the project seems overwhelming and you don't know where to start, so you procrastinate as much as you can. Sound familiar? Yup, it's just like cleaning your house: a big, overwhelming project that's difficult to start because there's no end in sight. But you can absolutely tackle it the same way you've learned to deal with your messy house: a little bit at a time.

When you're trying to figure out how to get started on a school or work project and you're too overwhelmed to just get going, try breaking it down into smaller chunks, and start working on the easiest one. Figure out what you can do that's not too difficult and doesn't require a huge time investment, and do that first. Even if it's not the first thing that needs to get done chronologically, it'll help get you past the block keeping you from getting started, and it'll get you into the groove of your project without jumping into the difficult stuff right off the bat.

From there, **you can 20/10 your way to a finished project.** Just continue working on the smaller parts until you've wrangled them into submission and your project starts to take shape. As with housework, doing a little bit at regular intervals will get you so much further than trying to do everything all at once. A marathon mentality is counterproductive in just about every circumstance (except, of course, actual marathons, but even then, you need to rest periodically during training). Switch to a mindset of "a little at a time" and find yourself starting to make some measurable progress.

Students can hugely benefit from 20/10s in all sorts of ways. Depending on how long you've been in school and how much academic autonomy you're used to having (or not having), coursework can be difficult to wrap your mind around. It's hard to get started, it's hard to get motivated, and it's really hard to keep going when there are a million other things you'd rather be doing. So many people find the hardest part of advanced coursework to be finding the drive to actually do it. And, as we find when dealing with our homes, we can attack schoolwork using some familiar concepts.

- **SET TIME ASIDE.** You need to schedule in your schoolwork so you make sure you're giving yourself adequate time to do it. It's very easy to say, "I'll get to it later," but before you know it, "later" has come and gone and you haven't done one single thing. Set an alarm to designate the beginning of your work session, and make sure you're not occupied doing other things that will prevent you from starting on time.

- **START EARLY.** Big paper, exam, or project coming up a ways from now? Start now. Even if you can only do some preliminary work or an outline, that's great! It'll need to get done at some point, so why not get the basic stuff out of the way so you aren't stuck doing it all at the last minute? Cramming is essentially the school version of marathon cleaning: exhausting, overwhelming, unsustainable, and incredibly common. By pacing yourself and starting early, you'll avoid the trap of the stressful all-nighter cram session.

- **BREAK IT DOWN.** When you're facing a giant, overwhelming project, first figure out what steps need to be taken in what order. That list or outline will provide you with a handy to-do list for getting things done. With some simple planning, you can give yourself a series of small, easily achievable tasks in the order you need to complete them.

- **WORK CONSISTENTLY.** One big schoolwork session, much like marathon cleaning, isn't going to be that helpful for you in the long term. Make yourself work a little bit every day, if for no other reason than to stay in the habit of working. As a bonus side effect to building the habit, you'll get a whole bunch of work done, too!

- **TAKE A BREATHER.** Just like when we're cleaning, we need to give both our minds and bodies a little bit of rest before moving on to the next thing. When you're cramming or scrambling to finish a project, you aren't allowing yourself any downtime when you aren't immersed in the project (and probably incredibly stressed out). By scheduling in breaks, you allow yourself to shift your focus away, even for a short period of time, and you can go back to the project after your break with fresh eyes and without the frustration and aggravation that always develop when you work straight through.

All of these methods can be applied to whatever you're doing out in the workforce as well. Projects and presentations become much less obnoxiously overwhelming when you lay out the organizational framework and then accomplish small tasks with regular frequency to help you get everything done without sacrificing your sanity. The key is to start early, work often, and give yourself time in between to do other things, work related or not.

SCHOOLWORK, HOUSEWORK, AND work projects are all work. They all require effort and concentration and at least a basic level of organization. But everything tends to become far more manageable when you stop looking at the big terrifying forest and take a nice long look at the trees. Once you start to get your home in order in a way that makes sense and is pretty easy for you, you'll be able to use all of those skills, habits, and routines in other parts of your life, too.

5

CONCLUSION

Now What?

UfYH Fundamentals

NOW WHAT?

With any luck, in the time it's taken you to read this book, you've not only started to make some small but positive changes in your habits, but you've also started to change the way you think about cleaning in general and how it relates to you specifically. After what is often a lifetime of hating or even fearing cleaning, it can be difficult to realize that it doesn't have to be something to fear or resist, and that you can, in fact, learn how to interact with your home in a way that makes it comfortable for you to live in. You can reshape the way you approach cleaning, organizing, and housekeeping so that it feels less like something you have to do against your will, and more like something you do for yourself, your health, and your well-being.

It's important to acknowledge that reading a book and making some changes, even if they're big ones, isn't an automatic recipe for lifelong success in keeping your mess under control. **There's no magic solution to the problem of disorganization,** and every possible way of dealing with it involves effort and motivation, even if it's just a little at a time. Don't expect to get your entire home clean and then never have a problem with it ever again. Here's a fundamental part of human nature: It's difficult for us to change. And we spend a lot of time looking for the miracle that's going to change us, only to be disappointed when human nature wins out and change proves harder than we hoped. The only way to really succeed is to not give up at the first setback (or the second or fifth or tenth), and to keep trying until it sticks. It might take longer than you'd like, but lasting, sustainable change is never immediate. It takes time, and it takes effort, and fixes are rarely permanent.

So you might backslide into your old messy ways. That's OK. It really is. It doesn't mean you're a failure, or you're a bad person, or all your hard work was for nothing. What's more important than finding yourself back in a disaster area of a home is what you do *after* that happens. With time and effort, you'll have developed the skills and motivation to be able to start back up again, no matter how small-scale, by doing a little bit every day to get that mess back under control. You can start and restart as often as you need to. Part of the cleaning-and-housekeeping continuous cycle is that you will always have the opportunity to try again, regardless of how long it's been or how much you need to catch up.

Don't beat yourself up if you find yourself falling into old habits (or the lack thereof). The really great thing about incremental change is that you can always start again from the beginning without having to upend your entire life. Feeling like a failure is never any fun, but just remember that each day just gives you another chance to start. If you fall behind for a while, it doesn't mean you've failed forever. It just means it's time to rediscover 20/10s and to start refocusing on those small but important habits like keeping up on the dishes, putting things away instead of down, and clearing off your flat surfaces. **The biggest step you can take is to just get started.** Even twenty minutes of work is a step in the right direction, and then later today or tomorrow or next week, you can do another 20/10, and another, and before you know it, you'll be back on track toward getting your household chaos back under control. It's not impossible, and it's not more than you can handle. You just need to get started and do that first 20/10.

Being successful with cleaning and housework is not a pass/fail situation. It's a constant cycle, an evolution of skills and motivation that will ebb and flow as time goes on. Sometimes, you'll be really motivated and put in consistent effort and be incredibly happy with your results. Sometimes, you'll be tired or sick or overworked and just not feel like it. And at those times, your effort is going to be minimal, and your results are going to be a little disappointing. One "bad" cycle doesn't mean you've failed or you're terrible at this, any more than one "good" cycle means you've reached the housekeeping pinnacle and you're done forever. Acknowledge all this domestic stuff as a journey with an ever-changing starting point and finish line.

If everything seems overwhelming, and you don't know where to start and you're not even sure you want to try, remember that you are not beyond help and that you are better than your mess. You deserve to live in a home that's comfortable for you, that you're proud of and enjoy, and that you can invite people into if you want. You can work on your relationship with cleaning, how you interact with the people you live with, and how you judge yourself and your home, until you're in a place where you're satisfied with all of those things. You can always improve, whether that means cleaning more often, cleaning more efficiently, streamlining your possessions, or communicating your way to an equitable division of household labor in your home. Once you stop thinking of your level of messiness as part of your personality, you give yourself the flexibility to change it. If you no longer say "I'm a slob" like it's something undeniably true and unchangeable, you allow yourself a whole lot of room to change what you thought of as part of your identity. "Messy" isn't who you are; it's a result of what you do or don't do, and it can change. You can change it.

Change is difficult, but the more open you are, the more successful you're likely to be. And you can measure success however you want! You don't have to compare how you stack up to someone else's expectations or some arbitrary standards that have nothing to do with you or your life. You might not think clearing off one countertop or putting one load of laundry away is a huge accomplishment for most people, but if you're proud of having done it, count it as a success. When things start feeling overwhelming again—and they probably will, because we're all human beings and we have a lot of shit going on—remember to treat yourself kindly, to forgive yourself for your perceived failures, and to celebrate every accomplishment, no matter how insignificant it might appear. No matter how bad things seem, no matter how much work needs to be done, you can do it. One 20/10 at a time.

UFYH FUNDAMENTALS

No matter where you are in the process of getting your mess under control—just getting started, trying to maintain, or even just beginning to think about making a change—keep these basics in mind, which make up the core of the Unfuck Your Habitat system and can give you an easy framework to fall back on if things start getting overwhelming.

- **TWENTY MINUTES IS NOT A LONG TIME.** Marathon cleaning sessions, while satisfying, are exhausting and make you never want to clean ever again. Twenty minutes at a time, once or a few times a day, is a sustainable way of keeping your habitat unfucked.

- **PUT IT AWAY.** Probably 75 percent of our mess is made up of things we didn't put away. Whether it belongs in a drawer, in the closet, in the trash, or in the cabinet, make sure it finds its way home. This is critically important in two areas especially: laundry and the dishes. Doing laundry and doing the dishes are not difficult tasks, but most of us give up before the putting-it-away step. Don't. As soon as you're done, everything goes back to its home.

- **MOST OF THE REST OF OUR MESS IS BECAUSE WE HAVE TOO MUCH STUFF AND NOT ENOUGH PLACES TO PUT IT.** This can be solved with either less stuff or more storage, and less stuff is generally the way to go.

- **GET OFF YOUR ASS.** Look, housework is a pain in the ass, and it's rarely fun. No one is disputing that, but it isn't **hard.** What is hard is overcoming your own lack of motivation and just getting up and doing something. Anything.

- **TIDY UP YOUR TOPS.** When your flat surfaces are clear, you feel like you're making serious progress. Counters, tables, dressers, nightstands, etc. Try it.

- **YOU DO NOT HAVE TO UNFUCK EVERYTHING ALL AT ONCE.** In fact, you shouldn't. That's how burnout happens. One thing at a time.

- **TAKE BREAKS.** It's important for your state of mind. You can integrate cleaning into everything else you do. It doesn't have to be all or nothing.

- **YOU CAN ONLY CHANGE YOUR OWN HABITS.** If you're dealing with roommates or spouses or kids or parents who aren't on board, the best you can do is tell them what you're doing (trying to keep ahead of the mess), and ask them to help not make it worse. Getting passive-aggressive or resentful because other people aren't playing along only hurts you, and it's not good for your brain.

- **A LITTLE EFFORT NOW SAVES YOU A LOT OF WORK IN THE LONG RUN.** That's why I advocate getting your stuff together at night for the next morning. That's why I like dumping some cleaner in the toilet or tub or sink and letting it start to work while I do something else. That's why taking the extra five seconds to wash your fork or put it in the dishwasher will always be a good idea, because it'll stop Dish Mountain before it starts.

- **STOP MAKING EXCUSES.** Yes, yes, you have a million valid reasons why your mess has taken over. But I refuse to believe that you can't spare twenty minutes, once a day, toward improving where you live. If you're still making excuses, you don't really want to do it. If you realize that twenty minutes is really no big deal, I can pretty much promise that things will get drastically better pretty quickly.

Addendum: If you are someone dealing with physical limitations, chronic illness, chronic pain, mental illness, or any other situation that makes getting your living environment under control difficult, please know that you are not lazy, and that "getting off your ass" may not be easy or even possible sometimes.

I encourage anyone who has limitations to modify challenges, suggest alternatives, and, above all, put your health first. If you can only do five or three minutes of unfucking, that's worth celebrating.

Most important: *Do what you can.* Some days, this might not be as much as you'd hoped. That's OK. Even tiny progress is still progress, and small but consistent change is more important than overnight miracles. You can do this.

CLEANING
CHECKLISTS

H ere are some handy UfYH-approved checklists for you to use as a guideline for daily, weekly, monthly, and seasonal cleaning. Copy these onto a piece of paper or whiteboard, or tap them into your smartphone— whatever is easy to access and hard to ignore. You can also go to UnfuckYourHabitat.com to download and print ready-made PDFs. Use the blank lines to write in your own chores/tasks as needed.

Unfuck Your Habitat daily checklist

- ☐ **Make your bed**
- ☐ **Wash the dishes**
- ☐ **Put your clothes and shoes away**
- ☐ **Deal with all incoming mail**
- ☐ **Wipe down kitchen and bathroom counters**
- ☐ **Clean litter box (if applicable)**
- ☐ **One or two 20/10s on an area that needs it**

_____

_____

_____

_____

_____

_____

_____

_____

_____

_____

_____

_____

Unfuck tomorrow morning . . . tonight!

☐ Wash the dishes in your sink

☐ Get your outfit for tomorrow together, including accessories

☐ Set up coffee/tea/breakfast

☐ Make your lunch

☐ Put your keys somewhere obvious

☐ Take your medication/set out your meds for the morning

☐ Charge your electronics

☐ Pour a little cleaner in the toilet bowl (if you don't have pets or children or sleepwalking adults)

☐ Set your alarm

☐ Go to bed at a reasonable hour

_____

_____

_____

_____

_____

_____

_____

_____

_____

Unfuck Your Habitat weekly checklist

☐ Wash sheets

☐ Vacuum/mop/sweep all floors

☐ Wash, dry, and put away laundry

☐ Wipe down stovetop and oven door

☐ Clean toilet

☐ Clean shower/bathtub

☐ Take trash out

☐ Wash all towels

☐ Put away everything on bedroom floor

_____

_____

_____

_____

_____

_____

_____

_____

_____

_____

_____

Unfuck Your Habitat monthly checklist

- ☐ Dust all surfaces
- ☐ Wipe down or vacuum baseboards and windowsills
- ☐ Clean out refrigerator
- ☐ Wipe down bathroom walls
- ☐ Clean light switches and door handles
- ☐ Throw away old magazines; shred or file old bills and mail
- ☐ Clean out and organize pantry
- ☐ Vacuum mattress

_____

_____

_____

_____

_____

_____

_____

_____

_____

_____

_____

_____

Unfuck Your Habitat seasonal checklist

☐ Wash curtains/clean vertical blinds

☐ Sort through clothes; donate/repair as needed

☐ Vacuum/clean upholstered furniture

☐ Clean oven

☐ Clean out bathroom drawers and cabinets

☐ Rotate mattress

_____

_____

_____

_____

_____

_____

_____

_____

_____

_____

_____

_____

_____

RESOURCES

There's no shame in needing a little helping hand when it comes to cleaning basics—how to clean a room, what order to do steps in, all the little things you might overlook. It may seem like these are things you *should* already know, but it's never too late to acquire useful knowledge about basic stuff. So here's a collection of helpful how-to's for unfucking your habitat. Keep in mind that there's more than one way to do things right, so consider these lists a starting point until you develop your own way of doing things.

Top ten general tips

1. Laundry and dishes have three steps: wash, dry, and *put it away, goddammit*. Don't consider the task complete until everything is put away. Otherwise, you'll find that clean clothes will live indefinitely in the dryer or laundry basket, and clean dishes will take up space in the dish drainer or dishwasher until it's time to turn them back into dirty dishes.

2. Direct sunlight will clear up mustiness in almost anything. If something's smelling a little musty and weird, just stick it outside for a few hours on a sunny day. (Make sure to bring everything back in before it rains or nature starts to have its way with your stuff.)

3. Denture tablets are awesome for cleaning water bottles or stained teacups. Just drop one in, fill with water, let it sit a bit, and rinse.

4. If you have a ridiculous amount of paper to shred, most office supply stores will shred for you (they charge by the pound), and many places have "community shreds," where you bring your stuff and they shred it in front of you, either for free or a nominal charge. Google "community shred [your area]."

5. Before you start cooking, fill your sink with hot soapy water. Chuck your prep dishes in as you go. (Except knives. Leave those off to the side.) Once your food is cooking, wash up! Clean as you go, so you can actually enjoy what you've cooked instead of dreading the huge pile of stuff to wash.

6. Sew ribbons on the corners of your duvet and the inside corners of your duvet cover, and tie them

together to prevent your duvet from migrating (and to make putting the cover back on after washing easier!).

7. Don't put it down, put it away. The extra few second or minutes you spend returning something to its rightful home will save you a bunch of time and aggravation later.

8. Take pictures! Your brain doesn't always "read" everything that's in a room when you look at it, but a picture will let you notice things you might have otherwise missed.

9. Do the stuff you're dreading the most first. You'll feel like a rock star.

10. Bring your empty hangers with you when the dryer's done. Hang stuff up right from the dryer. Don't give it the chance to languish in the laundry basket.

How to clean a bathroom

- Fill the sink with hot water and the cleaning solution of your choice.

- Pour a little cleaner in the toilet bowl.

- Spray the shower walls and bathtub with cleaner.

- Put away anything on the countertops and on top of the toilet tank, and anything that's out of place on any shelving.

- Gather up towels, washcloths, and the bath mat, and put them in the wash.

- Turn off the lights and fan (if you have one), and wipe down light fixtures and the fan vents with a barely damp rag.

- Clean out wherever you keep your toothbrush and toothpaste, and wipe down any other fixtures.

- Wipe down the fronts of all cabinets and drawers.

- Wipe down the countertops.

- Wipe down the toilet tank and the outside of the toilet, including the flush knob.

- Wipe down the toilet seat and then throw away or wash whatever you used to do that.

- Scrub the toilet bowl.

- Wipe down the shower walls and bathtub and rinse with the shower. Wipe dry.

- Put out clean towels, washcloths, and bath mat.

- Empty the trash can.

- Sweep the floor and then mop it.

How to clean a kitchen

- Gather up all dirty dishes and put them in a sinkful of hot soapy water to soak. If you have more than one sinkful of dishes, just get them all to the same general area.

- Collect and throw away all trash and recycling.

- Wash one sinkful of dishes.

- Start at one end of a counter and put everything away that doesn't belong. Keep moving from one end to the other and then on to the next counter.

- Put away the first load of dishes and then wash more dishes.

- Spray down the cooktop surface with a mild cleaner and wipe it clean.

- Put away more dishes and keep washing whatever is left.

- Wipe down the front of the oven, microwave, and other appliances. Wipe out any spills or crud in the oven.

- Go through your fridge and freezer and throw out anything expired or gross. Wipe down the shelves and drawers. Organize what's left in a way that makes sense: making more commonly used items the most accessible.

- Back to dishes if needed.

- When you're done with dishes, wipe out the sink.

- Wipe down all countertops.

- Change out dishcloths, towels, and sponges.

- Sweep the floor, then mop with hot water and cleaner. Work in a way that keeps you from having to walk on an already mopped spot.

How to clean (just about) any room

- Start from the top and work your way down. Dust falls, and the floor should be the last thing you clean.

- Collect all trash and recycling and put them in the appropriate place.

- Gather up any dishes and wash them.

- Pick up all laundry. Put clean clothes away and dirty clothes in the hamper.

- Start with the largest flat surface (counter, table, etc.) and put everything away. Take care not to just relocate the mess; instead, put things away in their proper homes. If something doesn't have a home, find one.

- Repeat for all other flat surfaces.

- Pick up everything off the floor. Start with the largest pile or worst area and keep working until the floor is clear of everything that doesn't belong there.

- Dust anything that needs dusting, starting with higher surfaces and working your way down.

- Sweep and mop or vacuum the floor.

Spring cleaning for actual people

- Keep washing your damn dishes.

- Open a damn window.

- Anything fabric that isn't clothes and can go in the washing machine? Wash it.

- What's that gross shit stuck to the floor over there? Wipe it up.

- It's warm outside now, so take all your goddamn trash out.

- Do you have a vacuum? Well, it's not doing you any good just sitting there. Use it. Use it on anything you can: floors, walls, weird spaces under things. Don't use it on your pets. They get cranky.

- Is something in your fridge possibly gaining sentience? Throw it out.

- How long has that light bulb been burned out? Just change it, for crying out loud.

- Change the batteries in your smoke detectors, because fire is a terrible way of dealing with a mess.

- No, but seriously. Keep washing your damn dishes.

Ten things you forget to clean: Kitchen edition

1. The grease and dust on the stove hood and fan filter.

2. The water reservoir of the coffeepot or teakettle.

3. The rubber seals on the fridge and freezer doors.

4. Inside and under fridge drawers and compartments.

5. Cabinet doors and drawer fronts.

6. All the interior surfaces of your filtered water pitcher.

7. The dishwasher filter.

8. The crumb tray and interior of the toaster.

9. That horrifying space between the counter and the stove.

10. Inside the light fixtures.

Ten things you forget to clean: Bathroom edition

1. Around the sink and shower faucets and knobs.

2. The walls (especially around the toilet).

3. The toothbrush holder and other containers.

4. The outside of the toilet/tank.

5. The hardware and surface of the toilet paper holder and towel bar.

6. The shower curtain and shower curtain liner.

7. The shelves of the medicine cabinet and other storage.

8. Under all of the bottles and other items in the shower.

9. All the corners of the floor, baseboards, and where the floor meets the fixtures.

10. Inside the light fixtures and exhaust fans.

Ten things you forget to clean:
Rest-of-the-house edition

1. Dusty fans and air conditioners.

2. Light fixtures and light bulbs.

3. Door handles, light switches, and outlet covers.

4. The tops and backs of couches and chairs.

5. Filters for air conditioners, dehumidifiers, and air purifiers.

6. Ceiling fan blades, where the ceiling meets the walls, and high windows.

7. Outdoor furniture and fixtures.

8. The inside and outside of trash cans, and the walls behind trash cans/recycling containers.

9. Remote controls, touch screens, keyboards, and other electronics.

10. The tops of windows, door frames, and molding.

Ten uses for vinegar

1. Drain volcano! (Pour baking soda down drain. Pour vinegar over it. Watch magic happen.)

2. Add a cup to your laundry to get rid of musty odors and fabric softener buildup, especially on towels.

3. Microwave a bowl of vinegar and water to make cleaning the inside of your microwave a zillion times easier.

4. Run your dishwasher empty except for a cup filled with vinegar, face up, to get rid of stains, smells, and mildew.

5. Descale your coffeepot or teakettle.

6. Take the sting out of sunburn. No, seriously.

7. Clean your fridge, especially the cruddy rubber seals.

8. Boil a pan of vinegar and citrus on the stove to get rid of lingering stink.

9. Kill weeds. (Will also kill plants that are not weeds, so use carefully.)

10. Put it in a spray bottle and use it to clean *everything*.

Dividing up the work: Talking points for difficult conversations with people who live together

- What chores do you each really hate? Is there overlap between those hated chores?

- What tasks don't you mind so much? Is it one of the other person's hated tasks? Once you've listed out what you each hate, like, or are ambivalent about, you can divide tasks up more equitably so no one's doing more than their share of stuff they hate.

- What needs to get done on a regular basis? How often, specifically, is "regularly"? Is anything time-sensitive or does it need to get done on a certain day?

- What needs to get done that currently isn't? Now is the best time to be honest about any holes in your current housekeeping.

- How long does each task take, and how often does it need to get done? What's the "grace period" for accomplishing a particular task?

- When is the best day/time to fit tasks into your schedule?

- How do you want to handle accountability? What's the plan for addressing things that aren't getting done?

- How should you handle the other person's stuff? Is there a preferred plan for working with or around a mess you didn't make?

Conversation Start-up Kit: Things to Say Before, During, and After the Cleanup

If you're the person who's asking for help:

- "I'm a little overwhelmed with trying to clean up my house. I could use some help if you can spare a few hours."

- "I'm pretty embarrassed by all of this, so it might be a little difficult for me. I appreciate your patience."

- "Can we start small? Maybe just the trash and dishes and then go from there?"

- "I just want to prepare you that going through Nana's knickknacks is going to be hard for me. We might need to take it slow when we do that."

- "My shoe collection is off-limits this time around. Maybe we can work on that sometime in the future."

- "Can we set up some time a few weeks out to reset some of what we've worked on?"

- "Once we're done, could you check in with me once or twice a week to see how I'm doing with it?"

If you're the person who's helping:

- "What am I not allowed to do or touch?"

- "Is there anything you think you can't handle that you'd like me to deal with instead?"

- "Do you need to take a break?"

- "Have you eaten/slept/had some water?"

- "I'm really proud of you. I know this isn't easy."

- "Do you want or need some help once we're done with this to help keep things organized?"

ONLINE RESOURCES

Support for hoarders/children of hoarders

Institute on Compulsive Hoarding and Cluttering: mentalhealthsf.org/programs/ichc/

Children of Hoarders: childrenofhoarders.com /wordpress/

International OCD Foundation: hoarding.iocdf .org/

Organizational desktop extensions

Fences (Windows only): stardock.com/products/fences/

Rainmeter (Windows only): rainmeter.net/

GeekTool (Mac only): tynsoe.org/v2/geektool/

General cleaning and other home resources

Unfuck Your Habitat: unfuckyourhabitat.com/

Unfuck Your Habitat blog: unfuckyourhabitat.tumblr.com

University of Illinois Extension Stain Solutions Database: web.extension.illinois.edu/stain/

Apartment Therapy: apartmenttherapy.com/

Useful general life advice

Adulting: adultingblog.com/

Captain Awkward: captainawkward.com/

You Need a Budget: youneedabudget.com/

Ask a Manager: askamanager.org

ACKNOWLEDGMENTS

This book could not have happened without all of the incredible people around me:

Mom, Dad, Aline, Gale, Judy, Dave, and the rest of my family, not only for teaching me these things so I can blather on about them to others, but also for unquestioningly supporting everything I've ever done.

My agent, Kurestin Armada, and my editor, Courtney Littler, for taking a chance, and who both showed me unending patience and constant support, and neither of whom complained even once about having to hold my hand through the most basic stuff imaginable.

My friends, who are the very foundation of the house that eventually became UfYH, who have acted as a support group, a cheerleading squad, a focus group, and occasionally group therapy, and without whom, there would be no UfYH at all. Everyone who let me bounce ideas off them or vent—online, over drinks, while walking the dogs, or through a series of increasingly panicked texts.

The Shulls, for everything they've done and continue to do

with the app, the site, and helping to shape UfYH in the early days and now.

Every person who has submitted a before-and-after picture or shared their story to UfYH, for your bravery in showing the world your homes. Everyone who has done the mini-challenges of unfucked their weekend, everyone who has posted about their first ever 20/10 or put five things away because social media told you to—the first step is always a big one.

And my husband, Andy, who has never doubted me, who understands and respects my need to retreat into silence from time to time, and who keeps the dogs occupied when all they want to do is use my laptop as a surfboard. None of this would exist without you.

INDEX